Tell Me True

TELL
ME
TRUE

Memoir, History,

and Writing a Life

Edited by

PATRICIA HAMPL

and ELAINE TYLER MAY

BOREALIS
BOOKS

Borealis Books is an imprint of the Minnesota Historical Society Press.

www.borealisbooks.org

The Minnesota Historical Society Press is a member of the Association of American University Presses.

Manufactured in the United States of America

10 9 8 7 6 5 4 3 2 1

∞ The paper used in this publication meets the minimum requirements of the American National Standard for Information Sciences—Permanence for Printed Library Materials, ANSI Z39.48-1984.

International Standard Book Number
ISBN 13: 978-0-87351-630-3
ISBN 10: 0-87351-630-3

Library of Congress Cataloging-in-Publication Data

Tell me true : memoir, history, and writing a life / edited by Patricia Hampl and Elaine Tyler May.
   p.   cm.
   ISBN-13: 978-0-87351-630-3 (cloth : alk. paper)
   ISBN-10: 0-87351-630-3 (cloth : alk. paper)
   1. Autobiography.   2. Biography as a literary form.   3. History in literature.
4. Truth in literature   I. Hampl, Patricia.   II. May, Elaine Tyler.
   CT25.T448   2009
   809'.93592—dc22   2008016607

Contents

Tell Me True

PATRICIA HAMPL & ELAINE TYLER MAY

Introduction

So what's the story? That homely question isn't seeking mere entertainment, certainly not fiction. It's asking for the truth. Or at least, a reasonable rendition of facts, reliable strands of information. But once this search produces a narrative, truth reveals its essential malleability in the face of storytelling. Writers of nonfiction face this conundrum daily. It's an occupational hazard—and an occupational fascination.

Memoir and history regard each other across a wide divide. In effect, they're goalposts marking the extremes of nonfiction. The turf that separates them—and of course connects them—is the vast playing field of memory. Though both forms are narrative and require the storytelling arts, they reverse each other—memoir being personal history, while history offers a kind of public memoir. A tantalizing gray area exists where memory intersects with history, where the necessities of narrative collide with mundane facts. The record always retains blank spaces—whether the record emerges from archival sources or from personal memory. Onto that blank space writers in both genres bring the remnants of the past they select in telling their stories.

This space is the uncomfortable location where the historian and the memoirist do the work of interpretation and imagination. History properly claims the authority of documentary record. Memoir, especially in recent times, angles forward with strong claims for the individual voice. History charts the big picture, memoir offers the

3

intimate portrait. Like opposing teams on the same field they seem—and sometimes are—charging against each other.

And yet.

When a little girl's diary, faithfully kept in the threatened secrecy of her hidden life, stands as the greatest testamentary document to the worst recorded events of the twentieth century—we know postmodern readers, not to mention postmodern writers, have narrowed the space between private and public, between the writing of history and the accounting of a personal life. Authority has shifted from facts to voice. Not that one cancels the other. Nor is this shift simply bad news or good news, but a very complicated story in itself. That story—about the record of history and the voice of memoir, about the documents of an individual life and the articulation of a shared past—forms the puzzle the essayists in this collection attempt to address.

The writers here—historians, journalists, poets, and fiction writers—are also memoirists. They—we—are caught in this complex rhythm, not masters of it. That is the point of this collection. For it is right here, in the contemporary tango of history and memoir, that crucial questions of narrative authority in our times are being resolved. Or perhaps not "resolved," any more than the mysteries of the past can be "solved." We have gathered testimony from the field—of play, of battle, of the writing of history and the writing of a life—from practitioners who have to contend with these devilish problems at the level of the paragraph and the sentence. Consider these essays, then, as dispatches from the front lines. The front lines of narrative documentary writing in our times.

The evermore pervasive use of the first-person voice in forms of nonfiction—journalism, history, even biography—that were once pristinely shrouded in distant ("omniscient") third-person narration held aloft by citations and sources, is no small cultural shift. Who tells the story can be as crucial as the story told. What does it mean to the writing of history that the first-person voice has claimed new authority, that memoir is sometimes seen not as "material" for history, but as history itself? And what does it mean to literature that memoir has become the signature literary genre of the age? Where is fact? Where fiction? Where is the "truth" in the disputed ground of nonfiction storytelling? Where does documentary authority reside—in the footnote or the footprint?

History has always relied on personal documents. Nothing new there. Letters, diaries, even family account books and ledgers have long been the gold standard of authenticity in history writing. These are the most primary of primary sources. But when autobiographical writing claims historical rights of its own—not as a "source" but as an act of history—then the equation has changed. So too in literature, when the personal story claims the authority of nonfiction while clinging to the gripping suspense and charms of fiction. Where are readers to place their trust?

Every writer consciously (or even unconsciously) reaching from the margins to the center for political and social power instinctively presents the personal story—the memoir, in effect—as a radical document, to be read as personal *and* public. Surely the most important autobiographical work of mid-twentieth-century America is *The Autobiography of Malcolm X*. A personal story, but one properly read as history, taught as history. The women's movement in its various strands also gave rise to an astonishing array of memoirs in the late twentieth century and beyond. And the Holocaust and the Gulag have provided a vast bibliography of memoirs, so much so that they have created new fields of social and historical study rooted in autobiographical documents and personal testimony.

"The personal is political," the women's movement of the 1970s asserted with almost gleeful fervor. But with the rise of the memoir in the final quarter of the twentieth century, not only politics in the present, but the aloof enterprise of history began to take on a strikingly personal voice. Meanwhile the novel, for two hundred years the narrative sovereign of literature, began looking over its shoulder at the upstart memoir.

The question of documentary record and personal voice has even reached opinion pages and editorial columns usually reserved for questions of foreign policy and domestic concerns. It's almost impossible to imagine the novel, as a form, calling down stern oracular judgments from the editorial board of the *New York Times*. But the memoir has found itself there in recent times more than once, caught red-handed in fabrications by rogue autobiographers, bringing the entire genre into question. Historians, too, have recently been called on the carpet for playing fast and loose with the facts, or with the words of other scholars.

These tabloid-delighting occasions are only a faint indicator of the dynamic, often dismaying power of the first-person voice in our times. Who tells the story, in what diction (neutral? lyrical?), and from what point of view? Is the narrative self properly obscured or revealed? Whether adrift in the broken images of memory or immersed in archival shards, through interviews, investigative travel, sifting through forgotten family albums in a dusty attic or ferreting out the assiduously buried evidence of nations seeking to elude history's sniffing nose—writers of memoir and history struggle, sometimes unsure of what genre they're writing in, genres that seem to be up for grabs. The grabbing can get quite strenuous, and brings us to the very question: where does history stop and memoir begin? What are the rules of this game?

But of course it isn't a game. Nothing less is at stake than the search for our individual and shared truth.

These questions brought us together as editors from the two disciplines facing each other across the disputed space filled with events and memory—history and creative writing. During the spring of 2007, we were able to bring together all the essayists in this book from across the United States and England for a remarkable series of panel discussions and readings on the University of Minnesota's Minneapolis campus. The participants of those spirited gatherings were invited to write essays based on their commentaries and their experience as memoirists—each given, in a sense, the final word.

But there is no final word to the questions that brought us together then or that bring us together again in this volume. If these individual testimonials establish anything, it is the signal value of the exchange. We are not, after all, opposing teams stampeding to claim the same turf. The movement is far more intricate than that. Perhaps it is more useful to imagine memoir and history standing on opposite sides of a mesh net, the shuttlecock of meaning and interpretation flying back and forth. Our purpose here is to keep the volley going.

FENTON JOHNSON

The Lion and the Lamb
or
the Facts and the Truth: Memoir as Bridge

• • •

WITH AN EXCERPT FROM
Geography of the Heart: A Memoir

FROM *Geography of the Heart: A Memoir*

On a discouraging night not long after Larry's death, I wrote my next-older sister, who had herself helped a lover through his death from leukemia. "Tell me, O older and wiser sister," I wrote, "how long will this grief last?" Older and wiser, she wrote back: "Grief is never over. The time will come when you control your grief rather than the other way around. You'll draw upon those memories when you need and want them, rather than having them show up uninvited. But your grief will never go away, which is the way it should be. It and Larry are part of who you are."

I am a man of few landscapes. Twice I have moved away from San Francisco and twice I have returned, not because of its tolerance or its fog (though I value both) but because I wanted to be near old friends. Looking back, I see that I was trying to re-create in a big city something like the blood family among whom I'd been raised, where on each walk to school I passed two centuries of my genealogy lying in the churchyard.

Now I am not much past forty, but of those whom I returned to be near, many are dead. Even in this city of small neighborhoods, many of the men from whom I learned to respect myself will not unexpectedly round the corner some bright autumn afternoon; I run little risk of the pleasant dangers of random encounters with my past, except in the recesses of my heart.

These days I visit with those dead men, my friends and lovers, though (as my sister predicted) on my terms, not theirs. The imperative to live presses its demands and I comply. Though I commonly have vivid dreams, I seldom dream of them; I never dream of Larry, a fact that saddens me. Maybe after I finish this book, I tell myself, that will change.

But writing is a contemplative profession. In exchange for solitude and various financial and psychological insecurities, I am given the luxury to daydream, and when in midafternoon I release my mind to wander, this is the place it often chooses to visit:

A large grassy bank cradled in the oxbow bend of a river flowing through a deciduous place, curving past a hardwood forest of oak and hickory and walnut—the landscape of my childhood asserts itself, though here and there a redwood pierces this temperate forest's profile and the stream runs clear and gravel-bottomed; I have lived many years in northern California. Mitt-leaved sassafras in the undergrowth—the air smells of cinnamon as I push through. The riverbank is populated with men, men who have loved me and whom I've loved, and men whom I've wanted to love: men I wanted to date but hadn't the courage or time to ask; men who rejected me, men whom I rejected; men I saw only once, on an airplane, in a bar, on a crowded bus, on a nearly empty beach, in a foreign land, in a classroom, in a church. Many of them are surely ill or dead, but they are all here, sons of the mothers of the world, alive and full of joy on the grassy bank of my heart, here at the cusp of their lives and somewhere in their midst sits Larry, my Larry. Young enough still to be beautiful, old enough to know the meaning of the coolness beneath the sun's warmth; old enough to know that every shadow promises night; old enough to know death. I cross that river to join them. We are gathered by a river where we have knowledge of time outside of time, of death without death, and there on the grassy green bank of my east-west heart, in the endless low-slanting sun, we give ourselves over to making memory and remembering.

◆ ◆ ◆

The Lion and the Lamb
or the Facts and the Truth: Memoir as Bridge

In 1894, a rural Kentucky entrepreneur sold New York businessman A. W. Dennett the frontier log cabin in which he claimed Abraham Lincoln had been born almost a century earlier. To quote Mark Twain, who makes a cameo appearance in this story: How singular! Yes, and how lucky! since Dennett parlayed the cabin into a business, transporting it around the country for exhibition as the Lincoln birthplace. Each time the cabin was broken down and reassembled, it lost an inch or two to the process; after several years of touring, it was placed in storage, considerably worse for the wear.

Then a committee of leading Americans, among them Twain, President William Howard Taft, Ida Tarbell, William Jennings Bryan, and Samuel Gompers, came together in a campaign to build the cabin a suitable home. To draw up the plans, they engaged John Russell Pope, later the nation's leading neoclassicist, architect of the Jefferson Memorial and the National Archives in Washington, D.C.

Pope designed a Greek temple for the Kentucky woods, a massive structure of rose granite and marble rich in numerology (one step for each year of Lincoln's life; a column for each of the original colonies) but with a minor problem: the interior rooms were too small to accommodate the cabin. Pope designed his monument to house not a real log cabin but an imaginary cabin that conformed to his conception of Lincoln's humble origins. But the corpses of history must conform to their tombs, so the sponsors lopped off several more feet of the cabin in order to squeeze it into Pope's mausoleum.

I know all this because I was born in Kentucky, a few miles from the Abraham Lincoln Birthplace National Historical Park. Taking the word of its guides as gospel, I grew up believing that the cabin—now reduced to the dimensions of a good-sized backyard tree house—had been the first home of our most beloved president. Ever sensitive to tourists and taxpayers, the park service stood by the myth until enough time had passed, at which point it quietly recast its brochures in the passive voice, describing the cabin as "traditionally held" to be Lincoln's birthplace. Today its web page reads, "an early 19th century Kentucky cabin symbolizes the one in which Abraham Lincoln was born."

Is there meaning to be found amid the murky facts surrounding the mud-chinked cabin that a wily Kentuckian assembled from logs he claimed to have found scattered about the original Lincoln farm and that he sold to a gullible (or enterprising) Yankee businessman? If the highest aspiration of human culture—of science and art, history and memoir—is not fact but truth, where does the story of the Lincoln birthplace cabin fall?

I was born in the Kentucky hills in 1953, a peculiar historical moment in a peculiar historical place. In the late 1920s and 1930s my mother regularly saw movies at the small theater in the county seat;

at ninety years old she still warbles lyrics from the musicals of the day, a living testimonial to the power of music to aid and prompt memory.

Then she married my father and moved to the far reaches of the county, into a world of narrow valleys and steep ridges. The movie theater in the county seat closed, victim of television's explosive growth, but the television signals were not yet strong enough to reach our remote village. Well into the age of electronic media, I grew up with little access to television and none to film.

Instead I grew up hearing endless stories from the whiskey-making, hardscrabble culture of the Kentucky hills, stories that shaped me for life, a fact I learned as soon as I left for college. I would be sitting on the floor of the hallway of my freshman dorm at the high-toned California university where I'd come on scholarship, relating some childhood memory to my classmates. Their first response was disbelief, so impossible was it for them to imagine a world so far removed from the universally prosperous suburbia of their experience. But I knew how to tell a good story, and I kept my audience engaged until invariably a listener piped up, "Would you *please* get to the point!" "The point?" I asked, genuinely puzzled. Even then I understood that the telling of the story *was* the point, that the facts of the story mattered less than sharing the communion of the word, the telling and the listening as entry point to a world outside of linear time.

Beginning with the later prophets, in a remarkable transformation mapped out by philosopher and religious historian Mircea Eliade,* the Jews began to see time not as round but as linear. Previous peoples, including the Jews, had understood time as circular, in the way still characteristic of Asian religions and philosophies. In this circular interpretation, time is a continuous recycling of birth, life, death, and

---

† *The Myth of the Eternal Return: Cosmos and History*, trans. Willard R. Trask (1954; Princeton, NJ: Princeton University Press, 1971) and *The Sacred and the Profane: The Nature of Religion*, trans. Willard R. Trask (1959; New York: Harper & Row, 1961).

rebirth, the unending loop that Buddhism labels "samsara." People lived for and by eternal, ever-repeating cycles—the rising and setting of the sun, the waxing and waning of the moon, the sun's apogee and perigee at its solstices marking the changing of the seasons, the miracle and mystery of growth and decay, birth and death.

The cultivation of memory—most frequently through music and orally recited poetry—was an essential component of these preliterate cultures. Music and oral recitation were vehicles and prompts for memory, enabling storytellers to preserve and recall epic narratives. In doing so the speakers reinforced the circle of time, establishing the dependence of the current generation on those who came before as well as its responsibilities to those who would follow. Priests led their communities in rituals designed to propitiate the deities, thus ensuring that the circle of time remained unbroken. They memorized and performed their duties with precision, since the slightest variation from how things had always been done might displease the gods and goddesses and so incur their wrath.

In contrast, later Jewish prophets began to perceive time as leading to an end point. A messiah arrives to liberate the chosen people from their suffering; shortly afterward, the world ends in apocalypse. The damned are damned, the chosen people are saved, end of story, end of history. In contrast to the once universally held perception of time as round and recycling, these prophets placed the universe on a line. Time became not a circle but an arrow, and the Jews (and by process of inheritance, Christians and Muslims) saw themselves at its tip.

Who can say why those later Hebrew prophets arrived at this revolutionary change in perception? Perhaps it was the outcome of the Jewish defeat, enslavement, and exile in Persia, circumstances so desperate that they demanded rethinking the tribe's relationship to time. However the transformation came about, Eliade argues that the emergence of the perception of time as linear rather than circular offered a powerful alternative to the once omnipotent allegiance to tradition. More and more people came to measure their lives by the clock and the calendar rather than by the sun and the moon. Culture, which had offered a brake and a caution against change, began to dismiss tradition as dated and to encourage and celebrate the innovative. In his insistence on reason as a gift from God, medieval theologian Thomas Aquinas unwittingly facilitated the rise of empiricism, in which interpretations once taken for granted were required to demonstrate their validity through objective measurement. New disciplines were born, among them the social sciences (the designation is telling), which sought authority through facts and statistics. Historians abandoned their ancient role as moralists and became chroniclers and analysts. Progress became our most important product.

An astute critic notes that the most literate ancients possessed prodigious memories—Augustine peppers his *Confessions*, to offer one example, with references that demonstrate an encyclopedic and intimate recollection of Scripture. All the same, whether as scribbled notes or BlackBerries, as technology proliferated it took charge of remembering, and our capacity to remember atrophied like any unused muscle.

Writer William Dalrymple describes a recent, analogous transformation in the storytelling traditions of the Gujar tribes of Rajasthan, one of the more rural states of India:

> The Gujars are very often illiterate, and illiteracy seems an essential condition for preserving the performance of an oral epic. It was the ability of the bard to read, rather than changes in the tastes of his audience, that sounded the death knell for oral tradition. Just as the blind can develop a heightened sense of hearing, smell, and touch to compensate for their loss of vision, so it seems that the illiterate have a capacity to remember in a way that the literate simply do not.*

Cultures based in circular time are clearly capable of invention— the wheel, the plow, and the sword predate by millennia the rise of

---

* William Dalrymple, "Homer in India," *New Yorker*, November 20, 2006.

our conception of linear time. But these cultures did not privilege innovation. The Chinese invented gunpowder and moveable type but saw them as novelties. Societies required a linear consciousness of time to *exploit the full potential* (such an American phrase!) of the newfangled, with the result that one invention after another changed the world in the space of a generation. To our perception of time as linear, we owe the invention of penicillin and the atomic bomb; the liberation of oppressed peoples and the rise of Bible-thumping televangelists; the privileging of desire over duty, individual rights over community obligations.*

For most Americans, completing the transition away from story-telling and oral history to technology-based media has been if not painless at least organic. Immigration had already loosened ties to the past, and in any case popular culture is by and large American culture, with the images and types of mass media by and large drawn from prosperous white American lives.

But for peoples in tradition-based cultures, the avalanche of urban pop culture represents the obliteration of memory. They must let go of the chain of stories that joins them to their pasts in exchange for iPods and PCs—assuming they can afford them. They are being

---

* Urban sophisticates are fascinated by contemporary writing from less developed cultures in part because it so often portrays this transition from circular to linear time. In his poignantly titled novel *Arrow of God* (1964), Nigerian Chinua Achebe's priest-protagonist Ezeulu refuses to allow his people to harvest their ripening yams even though to delay the harvest—as tradition requires—will spoil the crop and lead to famine. For Ezeulu, to violate tradition is to betray his priestly responsibilities, breaking the circle of time and severing the link to all that has come before. In desperation the villagers convert to Christianity—a philosophy that permits and encourages progress; a philosophy of linear time. A generation later South African writer J. M. Coetzee's *Disgrace* (1999) portrays a white father and daughter forced to choose between the values of the progress-oriented culture of the cities and the circular culture of the tribal people among whom they have chosen to live. In America the memoirs, essays, and novels of N. Scott Momaday (Kiowa) and Leslie Marmon Silko (Laguna Pueblo) portray the dislocation of native peoples whose communities are islands of circular time surrounded by linear, progress-oriented culture.

asked—or more often required—to exchange allegiance to tradition for allegiance to global consumerism. Where once they could assume a more-or-less secure place in the intricate web of a traditional society, now they find they are useful to global capitalism only so long as they can turn a profit.

The structures of traditional cultures were often hierarchical and discriminatory, but they provided their members with meaning—and before and above all else people need and seek meaning. While the prospect of seizing control of one's individual destiny has irresistible appeal to so many people for whom tradition represents oppression, other, less adventuresome people prefer pattern and ritual and the reason for being these provide, even at the price of what we in linear, progress-oriented cultures perceive as their individual identities.

The increasingly fierce resistance of tradition-based societies to Western culture has its roots in the visceral fear that it represents the death knell for cultural memory. Political and religious dogma have become vehicles through which that fear expresses itself in violence.

In revisiting these thoughts, I see I have implied an artificial dichotomy between a linear, "masculine" time of history and a circular, "feminine" time of art; between a linear, "masculine" time of science and a circular, "feminine" time of religion. In fact these are symbiotic, existing in no duality, as Buddhism teaches. As evidence of their interdependence, I offer memoir, which rests one comfortable foot in the "masculine" world of history and its other foot in fabulous "feminine" fiction.

That is emphatically not to say that in writing memoir I fictionalize, i.e., that I make it up. In writing memoir only a hack makes it up. In writing memoir the rule of the game—the discipline that provides the vessel for memoirists' words—is our contract with the reader that our writing is as truthful to memory as we are capable of being and that we will let the reader know, directly or by implication, how reliable we feel ourselves to be. In *Angela's Ashes* Frank McCourt does not need to tell us that he is fictionalizing his description of the moment of his birth; he could hardly have been taking notes. In recalling his French governess in *Speak, Memory*, Vladimir Nabokov tells us up front that he "was not there to greet [Mademoiselle]"—but then he so vividly imagines her descent from the train amid the depths of the Russian winter that two sentences into his description we've forgotten that he's writing fiction. A lesser writer might have been content to leave us dazzled by sleight of hand, but Nabokov, ever the literary trickster, ends this gorgeous passage by gently reminding us that we've been had:

> Very lovely, very lonesome. But what am I doing in this stereoscopic dreamland? How did I get here? Somehow, the two sleighs have slipped away, leaving a passportless spy standing on the blue-white road in his New England snowboots and stormcoat. The vibration in my ears is no longer their receding bells, but only my old blood singing. . . . The snow is real, though, and as I bend to it and scoop up a handful, sixty years crumble to glittering frost-dust between my fingers.

The great memoirists do not conceal their uncertainties but use them as another tool for making art. They work both from empirically, historically verifiable fact and from the art of constructing and handing on the best of all possible stories. They work, in fact, in both linear and circular time.

Even now I write stories because to take up the pen is to remove myself from the linear time of calendar and clock and enter instead into circular time, the time of religion and philosophy and art, the time of eternity, the time of God.

Memoir is by definition a vehicle for subjectivity. The label gives notice to readers that they are entering the funhouse of individual memory, in which a great deal of the pleasure derives from the entry the writing affords into the writer's deepest consciousness. And paradoxically it is through subjectivity that one best gains access to truth, the enduring, timeless wisdom that enables us to have and keep faith in ourselves and in each other, in our collective capacity to live in harmony with each other and with our planet.

What distinguishes memoir from more conventional approaches to recording and analyzing experience? A friend offers an old saw— "The victors write history, the losers write their stories," a joke that contains a powerful truth: stories have a way of outlasting victories. If someone had told me when I was in my early thirties that I would publish a memoir shortly after I turned forty, I would have rejected the suggestion outright. Memoirs were something you wrote when you were old, after your hair turned gray, assuming you still had hair. And then HIV arrived in America and my partner died, and—motivated by the impulse to preserve his story and that of my community for those who followed—I wrote *Geography of the Heart* in response to the imperative of the historical moment. A universally familiar example makes the point more emphatically: millions more readers worldwide know the poignant story of Anne Frank's life in hiding than know the facts of Hitler's rise to power.

A successful memoir is not a product of the self-obsession of a selfish, me-first generation; it is evidence of literate people's recognition that the written word has replaced the story told by the winter fire as our means of establishing and preserving cultural memory.

Linear time is individual time, in which our first commitment is to ourselves, to our particular lives, achievements, and stories. Circular time is community time, in which individual interests are secondary to those of the family, tribe, or nation. Memoir arises from the intersection of these two ways of living through time. It conflates the empirically verifiable facts of history—the particular events that make up the linear time of calendar and clock—with the timeless, circular consciousness of art. Memoirists write in service not only to fact, though the facts are and must be our tools, but to truth. We are in service both to linear and circular time, to progress and eternity.

The same might be said of history, but only when its authors bow in Franciscan humility before the power of their pens—the power of the written word. Historians who abandon the illusory power of "objectivity"—who acknowledge forthrightly their perspectives and limitations—are submitting to the discipline of art and so to the discipline of truth.

We require the facts to form accurate formulations of the truth. Traditions founded in warm desert climates once forbade eating shellfish, probably because the risk of spoilage was so great; now we understand that with proper refrigeration the oyster can be our world. Once the imperative for tribal reproduction and the risks of sex and pregnancy forbade sexual activity except under highly restricted circumstances; now we have the means, if not the will, to control both reproduction and the physiological risks that accompany intimate contact. Disciplines that work from a linear understanding of time (e.g., science, conventionally produced history) provide facts with which we may test and retest our truths in an eternally changing world. Working from these facts, disciplines that subscribe to a circular understanding of time (e.g., fiction, poetry, religion) arrive at, evaluate, and modify our enduring truths. We are at a moment of utmost historical significance, where we have the combination of prosperity and historical perspective required to understand and practice this truth: Science and religion, history and art—these cannot and must not exist as dichotomies. Each way of being and seeing requires the other if it is to evolve and prosper.

The conception of time as linear enabled society to progress from the generations that preceded ours. It enabled our forbears to imagine a better world and then act to achieve it. Life is better now for so many people—as a gay man I count myself among them—because we liberated ourselves from the notion that because we had always lived a certain way we must continue to live that way forever.

At the same time, though I am the beneficiary and practitioner of reading and writing and am fully committed to the literate world, I imagine an ideal world where we could understand that the printed word does not fix the story on the page but makes it available to a new generation of interpreters. In my dreams we could retain access to the slow workings of circular time—the time of all those purveyors of oral tradition, our poets and storytellers and philosophers—while living by the linear time of the written word.

Paradoxically, technology may be our means to that end. Our cultural obsession with plagiarism originated with the invention of moveable type, which allowed for mass production of books and gave birth to the notion of intellectual property—the principle that an individual or corporation owns exclusive rights to the public life of an idea or story. For better or worse the Internet is dismantling that principle daily, as millions worldwide access and copy and modify others' work. As a writer with a financial stake in the process, I view this development with dismay, but as a storyteller I am intrigued by the prospect of millions of individuals reclaiming the right to shape and retell the old stories in ways that reflect the realities of their lives.

I begin my undergraduate creative nonfiction classes by telling students that facts are malleable, truth is enduring. "No, no," they cry, "it's the other way around." The semester becomes a process of demonstrating that facts, like statistics, can be manipulated to any variety of interpretations (recall the history of Lincoln's birthplace cabin), but truth proves itself across time. *Do unto others as you would have them do unto you. Energy is equivalent to mass times the speed of light squared.* These are overarching truths that prove themselves across generations of testing against the confusing and contradictory facts of experience.

Truth lies not in fact but in beauty; not in the cabin where Lincoln was purportedly born but in the longings for saints and profits that brought its logs to be found, assembled, and enshrined; neither in head nor heart alone but in the understanding that these are integrally intertwined and cannot be separated without doing violence to both.

. . .

Earlier I referred to the perceived opposition of science and art, history and myth, fact and fiction. The great promise of postmodern relativism lies in our understanding these as complements rather than opposites. As poet Alison Hawthorne Deming wrote, our new world is "not either/or but both/and." These disciplines must become not distinct and opposing but permeable and interpenetrating.

Already we have models in our most enduring thinkers and writers—too many to name, but as worthy representatives I offer Albert Einstein in science and N. Scott Momaday in literature: Einstein's writings include passages that read like mystical treatises, and Momaday incorporates anthropological research into his renderings of tribal history. The work of these thinkers and writers and those like them will endure because they actively cultivated a synthesis of science and art, history and myth. They propose to us a world which may respect and celebrate both individual rights and community obligations.

Memoir accesses both means of living through time, circular and linear, communal and individual. In doing so, the memoirist contributes toward healing the deepest wound of Western culture—that is, the artificial (if once useful) division between mind and body, head and heart, fact and truth. If we could understand and live through time as a spiral—the intersection of line and circle, containing and expressing both the facts of history and the truths of art—perhaps we could more competently create stories that enhance our capacity to live in harmony with each other and our fellow creatures.

A grand claim for what most perceive as a minor art, but we must begin somewhere, and where better than memoir? All human knowledge begins in our prodigious capacity to remember. This much is plain: the great challenge of the present century is not exterior but interior. At least for the moment, Western culture has conquered the planet. Now our challenge is to learn to live in harmony with our Earth, with each other, and with ourselves.

In a world in which the facts are so easily manipulated, what is truth, and how may we know and preserve it? Worldwide we are witnessing violence with its roots in the tension between science and religion, history and memory, the law and the heart, reason and faith. Extremists from both sides would have us believe that these forces are mutually destructive when in fact we are at a moment when we may draw upon and give expression to both, creating a synthesis and achieving what Zen Buddhists aptly call "nonduality."

Is it not the responsibility of the magicians of the earth—its artists and scientists and priests and writers—to propose and model peace? Perhaps memoir, a vessel so particularly well suited to embrace both the head and the heart, fact and truth, can provide us one means through which seemingly hostile disciplines can make constructive peace, in which the scientist will lie down with the priest, the historian with the fictionist, the lion with the lamb.

ANNETTE KOBAK

Whose War?

. . .

WITH AN EXCERPT FROM
Joe's War: My Father Decoded

FROM *Joe's War: My Father Decoded*

It was 1993, and I was visiting Australia again, this time to take a trip with my parents up to the Great Barrier Reef. . . . We drove through the lush, rolling hills behind Byron Bay and Brisbane, bathed in golden sunshine and almost English except for their sudden peaked, red, rocky hills. Then came the monotonous kilometres of sugar cane country, with their bulbous cane toads creeping around inside. We passed through endless creeks, their names spelling out bluntly the tale of men's first encounter with them . . . Kangaroo Creek, Duck Creek, Deadman's Gully, Magpie Gully, Spider Creek, Devil Devil Creek and even Creek Creek. I said I'd heard that to double a word in the Aboriginal language was a way of saying "very." My father laughed, and said he had a better idea, which is that they were deaf, and needed everything said twice.

He said this with fellow-feeling, because deafness by this time was beginning to be an issue. He'd been going slightly deaf for a while, which he put down to the noise of the Stuka and other bombings in the war, and the Morse code machines. It looked as if his corporal's sardonic prediction of going deaf "by the age of thirty" was belatedly coming true. What we all failed to notice for a long time, since my mother had an eccentrically extravert conversational style, was that she was going profoundly deaf as well. She felt that this, too, must have been a result of the war—of the Blitz—since deafness wasn't otherwise in the family. Just as communication had opened up between us, this new subtle impediment was brought in to hamper the kind of spontaneous, redundant remarks that are the stuff of life. . . . New kinds of no-go areas were threatening, and we would have to beware that what was said didn't become that much more two-dimensional than ordinary language, a kind of Morse code. Around the house notices had begun to appear: FAX SWITCHED ON? KEYS? WINDOWS LOCKED? I half expected SSHHH. WALLS HAVE EARS. My father had made a device on the telephone which made it ring far more loudly and shrilly than usual, and added a flashing red light, so that to ordinary ears a telephone call now felt like being hunted down by the police.

On the way up to Cairns we went to the usual tourist sites, visiting rainforests and crocodile farms. At one, we saw a keeper feeding a crocodile in a large pool. The crocodile, with its zigzag grinning jaw in its massive pugilist's head, ambled into one end of the murky pool, whiplashing its scaly tail behind, before disappearing under the brown water. The man took a dead chicken round to the other side of the now-still pool and held it out on the end of a stick. There was a long silence, then at the man's feet the waters erupted like a volcano and a prehistoric jaw rocketed out vertically to snatch it in one gulp. It was awesome, archetypal, and strangely emotionally familiar.

♦ ♦ ♦

Whose War?

Last week, over a coffee with an archivist at the Imperial War Museum in London, I asked him as an afterthought, "By the way, is there a . . . *penalty* for breaking the Official Secrets Act?" It was late in the day to have thought of this: my book about my father's secret life in World War II and beyond, *Joe's War: My Father Decoded*, had come out three years earlier, and the seventeen cathartic tapes he and I had made over the course of a few blazing hot Januarys in Australia—where my parents now live—had just been transformed by the archivist into seventeen gleaming CDs, one set of which was now lodged in the Imperial War Museum's sound archives.

The dutiful part of me felt proud that this record of my father's war, and of his early life in Czechoslovakia (where he was born) and Poland (where he studied), was preserved in such safe hands, for future searchers to consult or ignore, according to the vagaries of history to come. Proud, that is, until I asked that question. "Oh yes," the archivist replied, "there would be a prison sentence for breaching the Official Secrets Act."

Walking home to Borough with my set of the golden CDs—the new, boxed-up version of my father's life I thought how ironic it would be if, after all the perils my father had survived, he should in the final furlong find himself clapped into prison courtesy of his daughter.

Of course, I exaggerate. This won't happen: the secrets in question belong to sixty-one years ago; airing them has given unexpected insights into the history of World War II as well as of the Cold War; my father is well into his eighties now and lives on the other side of the globe; the very thought of *punishment* would be waved away airily by the powers that be, with graceful murmurs of appreciation for his defense of the realm . . . *wouldn't it?* All the same, the brush with the mere possibility of penalties reminded me that the truth telling of memoir comes at a price. For the project of memoir—the lone voice telling its tale—can rouse sleeping dogs that others would rather let lie. The tale told can, for example, conflict with the narratives of power; and power can be not too happy about that.

I had no thought of such things when I embarked on *Joe's War*. In fact, it took a while for me to be interested in my father's story at all. Like any child, I took my surroundings for granted: I didn't query my father's taciturnity, or the fact that we didn't have a telephone, or the fact that his eyes oscillated continuously, or that he slept with a hammer under his pillow. I was an only child, and we lived quite a cut-off life (that no-telephone, for a start) in an anonymous south London suburb, with few visitors, apart from the occasional sighting of one of my English mother's family. It didn't occur to me, even as an adult, that I had a childhood or story worth writing about: to look back on it was to see something formless and bitty, with more blanks than memories. "Memoir" was surely about settled, substantial people. It emanated from writers with provenance, with peopled childhoods and a sense of place, like Gwen Raverat and Nabokov. And my father's own backstory seemed more than an absence: it was a no-go area I obligingly didn't go into.

Until, that is, I started writing about my childhood in the guise of what was to be a fictional tale about World War II. By retrieving that hammer, those flickering eyes, and even that lack of a past from memory, I belatedly began to see that these things were not *normal*.

By this time I had teenage children of my own, and my parents had emigrated to the other side of the world. Why, I now wondered, did I know almost nothing about my father's life before he'd arrived in England in 1940 as a young soldier with the Polish army? And why hadn't I asked about it, in all the seventeen years I'd lived at home?

Partly, it was because at the time I'd put any peculiarities down to the fact that my father was foreign, with different ways—like drinking sour, curdled milk or making lime tea from limes he found on a tree (not using Brooke Bond and milk, like normal people!). I knew he'd been born in an obscure country called Czechoslovakia, notoriously a "faraway country" to Prime Minister Chamberlain in 1938, and once again faraway to us English after the war, behind its "iron curtain"; an iron curtain that was solid and metallic, in my child's mind. I'd also gathered that my father had been through a tough war, fighting as a very young and accidental soldier in the Polish army (why Polish, when he was Czech?) on the front line in France, being bombed from the air, hiding in haystacks. No wonder his eyes flickered. And I knew that all his family was now locked away behind that Iron Curtain (a piece of Churchill's inspired wordsmithery, although coined, I would find, with some bad faith, since he had such a hand in bringing it down). Early on, my father sent his family food parcels, but even that connection stopped, after it became too dangerous for them to have any contact with the West. Otherwise, he didn't want to talk about such things as I grew up, steering away from the no-go areas with (I now see) a subtle repertoire of stonewalling, jokiness, and well-pitched unavailability—the latter not unusual for fathers at that time, and in his case cloaked with the cover of his work (a researcher with the Coal Board) and solitary home tasks like carpentry and watch mending.

This much I'd known about my father—Józef, as he'd been born, then Joseph, as he'd been known in England, and now redubbed, with Australian chumminess, plain "Joe." And as a child it had been enough. My only interest in the war had been in zooming around bomb sites with the local children, wearing gas masks and pretending to be airplanes as we played "Japs and Germans"—with scant idea who "Japs and Germans" were. By adolescence, the grimness and conflict of war seemed to have been kicked into a different era by Bill Haley's "Rock Around the Clock" and the emerging swinging sixties. By university, the war was coming back retro, as I donned a flak jacket over my miniskirt. With marriage, and children, I became immersed in the present and future, not the past; and in the seventies the link with my father and the war receded even further, when he and my mother emigrated to Australia—on the face of it, for my father's work and a better quality of life. It wasn't until the eighties, when the warmth of Australia and the more forthright curiosity of the Australians thawed out my father's reserve, and when my marriage broke up, that I turned around and took stock of what I'd never asked him.

As I got wind of his story, I began to see that a Central European take on the war might look quite different from our standard British version of Churchill, Colditz, and the Dam Busters—and, more to the point, that I'd never heard or read one. I wanted to explore it, and my father, in a book. I wanted it to be about his journey to England across war-torn Europe in 1939–40, and my journey toward him. (I just mistyped this as "my journey toward *me*," and of course it was that too—what else is memoir?) The book was always going to be about history and emotion: both, interlaced. By now, I'd written my first book, a biography of a young nineteenth-century traveler, Isabelle Eberhardt, with a troubled Slavonic past full of family secrets she never knew about. My subconscious had evidently been working overtime, doing a recce of the territory that needed exploring.

Yet in 1988 the market wasn't ripe for memoir, let alone for one about an unknown individual from an obscure country like Czechoslovakia. As my American editor pointed out regretfully, since the U.S. president (Reagan at the time) didn't know even where Pakistan was, there was slim chance of finding readers interested in a remote country with an unspellable name. She also wondered how I could write frankly about my parents while they were still alive, and without "instrumentalizing" them—a new word to me—and at the time, before the memoir boom, these seemed good points. So the memoir went onto the back burner while I worked on another book, did a radio series on travel writers, and brought up my children.

But it simmered away in the background. When time and money allowed, I visited my parents in their new homeland, and with green curtains drawn against the midday sun, my father and I made those tapes, at first faltering, about a gray and fraught European time. And back home in England, I boned up on the history of Czechoslovakia, Poland, and World War II, to understand the complex context to his story.

These forays into history became riveting to me in their own right. I was discovering so much I hadn't known and that nobody seemed to know, whole narratives absent from the history books. I began to see a backdrop to Joe's story that he himself hadn't fully known, as a lone young individual hit suddenly by "the monster from outside," as his fellow Czechoslovak Milan Kundera called the history of the twentieth century. I began to see, too, how history might look like that monster if you'd been brought up in Central Europe in the thirties. My father and I pieced together the past, and bit by bit— especially after the Soviet Union collapsed in 1991—he dropped his guard.

Joe, it transpired, had been an eighteen-year-old engineering student in Lvov (then in Poland, now in Ukraine) when war broke out in September 1939 and Poland found itself partitioned overnight between the two tyrannies of Nazi Germany and Soviet Russia. Lvov fell to the Soviets, Stalin's Terror began, and Joe, picked randomly off the streets whilst queuing for scarce bread (scarce anything, shortages set in at once), managed to bribe his way out of prison just before he became part of a quota of Siberia-bound prisoners. Realizing that students and teachers were being targeted and that studying would no longer be safe, he made a perilous journey back to his parents' mountain village, now in Nazi-occupied Poland. The local vicar, knowing him to be a good skier who knew the terrain, asked him to take some refugees clandestinely across the Slovak border, and the third time he'd done this, the Nazi commandant in the village found out and put out a death warrant for him. In January 1940 he had to turn back on skis through the mountains, and he had never seen his parents again. (No wonder he had nothing from his past.) He described how he ended up joining the Polish army—under the French army, until that collapsed—in Marseilles and had found himself, as a raw recruit, fighting on the front (those bombs and haystacks), and then transported to the unknown country of England on the last ship out of occupied France. There he met my English mother, who was in the women's air force, and a few years later I was born.

Joe's memories, locked away for half a century even from my mother, came out pristine, like insect fossils trapped in amber. He had vivid recall of detail: of the Omega watch he gave to the young guard in the prison to set him free; the metal rod "15 millimeters by 30 centimeters" with which he'd killed an NKVD officer (or did he?); of the exact two suits, balaclava, overcoat, shoes, and galoshes he wore as he skidded across the frozen river San at night under gunfire to get back home; of the teeth of the smiling Senegalese soldiers amid the military chaos in France; of the Scottish coal-carrying tanker that rescued his unit; of Morse code, which his ear, brain, and fingertips can still transmute at high speed, like an automaton, from dots and dashes into the alphabet.

I was struck by the clarity of his recall, the exactitude of the detail. Perhaps, I thought, it was because he'd studied engineering and would become a physicist, a specifications man. But I came to see there was another reason for this specificity, too: he'd been traumatized by the relentless sequence of events hitting him in the nine dislocating months from September 1939 to summer 1940, when he reached England. In his state of high alert, everything was etched keenly on his memory. The amygdala, we're told—seat of the fight-or-flight impulses—registers things more deeply than the neocortex, engine of our more evolved selves. His silence at home had come from what we now call post-traumatic shock and from depression, exacerbated by being cut off from his family and homeland by the onset of the Cold War. And yet . . . there was more to it than that, too. It's not depression, after all, that makes you stash a hammer under your pillow.

By now, our conversations were taking place in a new century, the twenty-first. The monster-from-outside century, with all its wars, was, the dates told us, another era. Until, on September 11, 2001, the monster crashed in on us in the West, and it began to look as if it had merely gone in for some shape and place shifting. By now, my book had been commissioned in America and Britain, in the wake of the new vogue for memoir and of the opening up of the former Soviet Union. Place names like Czechoslovakia, Lvov, and Ukraine were not quite so alien any more; even presidents and prime ministers had heard of them.

Yet because I'd assumed, in my English island-dweller way, that my father was home and dry when he got to England, I hadn't asked much about this time. I got that wrong: it was precisely what had happened *after* he got to England that sealed his fate for the next half century and locked him into silence.

In 2000, Joe told me the last piece of the story: in 1941, after Russia became the unlikely ally of the western powers, he'd been drafted from his Polish army training camp in Scotland to a small Polish intelligence unit in London, a unit with such sensitive implications for the balance of power between the West and East that its existence had to be kept top secret. My twenty-year-old father, in a strange country and with little English, was given the job of transcribing the Russians' Morse code: spying on the Soviets. Our allies. It was not high-level espionage—and he had, of course, no option but to do it—but he was told by the officer in charge that the less he knew about the context of what the unit was doing, the better. Trust *no one.* (What, not even you? he asked the officer, who laughed and said: You'll do.) It was here he committed to that Official Secrets Act.

Trust no one. The instruction imprinted itself so vividly on his mind, in his vulnerable position in a foreign country, that he put the lid on all his experiences before and during the war. Rather than let anything out accidentally, he let nothing out. And no sooner was the war over than the Cold War began, and even my father, with his studied, almost belligerent lack of interest in politics (and I now see why), could see that the fact of the unit's existence—albeit in the past—became just as incendiary in a Cold War climate as it had been during the "hot" war. Perhaps more so.

His unit had been set up after the Russians switched sides in summer 1941, for with the Russians suddenly their allies' ally, the Poles were presented with a dilemma. They had good historical reasons to distrust the Russians: for having three times been party to the partitioning of Poland, and for having just brutally invaded part of their country in September 1939, in alliance with the Nazis. They also suspected that the Russians had designs on their homeland, now under Nazi control and chronically weakened through war, and they urgently needed to monitor their intentions toward it. Yet they couldn't do this openly, since this would jeopardize the alliance with the only power now capable of helping the West finish the war against the Germans. The British wanted to monitor their unlikely Communist bedfellows, too, but couldn't decently spy on allies, so were glad to let the Poles do the work for them—as long as neither side admitted to it, as long as it was kept secret. And neither side did admit to it, which is why I could find no mention of the unit in any history book. And why you still won't.

Unfortunately for the Poles, from the 1943 battle of Stalingrad onwards, Russia's hand in the war was strengthening. Roosevelt wanted to court this major force, and Churchill found he had to, with Britain itself now hemorrhaging money and power. Since the Poles in the West were beginning to be a hindrance to this courtship (although they were still fighting and winning battles for the allies), the two leaders secretly and treacherously dropped their cause at the Tehran conference in winter 1943 and then more openly at Yalta in spring

1945. The dire consequences for the Poles became clear in summer that year, as Churchill officially recognized the Soviet-installed government in Poland, withdrew support for the exiled Polish government in London, and—so shockingly to the Poles, as well as to their colleagues and friends in the other allied forces—did not invite the Polish forces to the victory celebrations in 1945 and 1946. In his own mind, my father now had nowhere to go, except to retreat into silence.

Like the other stranded Poles, he was now vulnerably stateless for years after the war, the years of my childhood, until he got, in that peculiarly English phrase, his "naturalization"—that is, his British citizenship. Stateless, he watched his homelands of Czechoslovakia and Poland lose their freedom to the very people he'd been spying on. He'd been dutiful and brave, as so many Polish servicemen and women had been, but he was now without security or nationality in a country that was cold-shouldering the Poles for internal reasons of its own (war weariness, unemployment, male envy of the dashing figure they cut in their smart uniforms, with women, the perverse flirtation with Communism by establishment figures like the press baron Lord Beaverbrook, or Etonian spy-traitors like Kim Philby and Guy Burgess).

In the fifties and sixties, Joe saw spy scandals detonating around him in Britain—George Blake, Gordon Lonsdale, Buster Crabb, John Vassall, the Profumo affair. In his own mind, he had every reason to fear the knock on the door in the middle of the night, small fry that he was. Hence the hammer under the pillow—a rather basic, but at least legal, weapon. Joe knew that most English people, blithely ignorant of police states, would have scoffed at his fears as melodramatic. Yet even now, half a century later—and technically after the Cold War has ended—these fears still have all too real currency, if the Russian Alexander Litvinenko can be poisoned in broad daylight in a central London hotel.

My father was no enemy of the Soviet Union—no enemy of any nation, just one of countless pawns of war—but his fears were not for nothing. To live in a police state, as he had done for a few months, and as many thousands of other Poles had done in far worse circumstances in Soviet labor camps—or, worse, and notoriously, shot at Katyn—and as hundreds of Czechoslovaks had done when Hitler turned their country into a "protectorate" (always, always beware that word), left you with a different frame of mind from island dwellers, even if they had suffered the Blitz. It was another gulf he bridged with silence. .

Many of his fellow Poles folded that silence around them too: over two hundred thousand servicemen and women from the three armed forces in Poland had fought to secure the freedom of Britain and countries in continental Europe—in Norway, France, the Battle of Britain (where the Poles' four squadrons, representing only 5 percent of the air force that defended Britain, famously accounted for 12 percent of enemy losses), the Battle of the Atlantic, Tobruk, Lenino, Monte Cassino, Ancona, Bologna and on D-day and at Arnhem. They were not only betrayed by their friends but, as I found to my surprise, until recently airbrushed out of the histories of the war. From Tehran onwards, the Polish government in exile and the Polish press in the West were gagged: the Polish ambassador to America wrote later, "We were asked to keep everything secret. We were deprived of the possibility of obtaining the support of public opinion. Our lips were sealed."

Their lips were sealed, and they were also emotionally stymied by not wanting to appear a victim and by their gratitude at having a home in a free country. With nowhere to put their anger, many turned in on themselves. Since *Joe's War*, I've had scores of letters from their children, all of whom felt they grew up in some twilight zone they couldn't figure out, dominated by the silently brooding presence of their Slav father (*The Quiet Slav* was the working title for the book, deemed a bit *too* quiet for the market). Most of the correspondents' fathers had died too young—of despair, the historian Adam Zamoyski told me; as his own father had done, even though (perhaps even because) he was descended from the Polish nobility.

And so my father's silence, and the odd details my memory had stored—the hammer, the nervous eyes—had led me into potent historical silences, ones glossed over for political expediency by the narratives of authority. For his part, Churchill soon felt a laudable guilt about the nations he'd helped commit to living in a police state, a guilt that he buried with words and silences of his own. Privately, in a cable to his wife, he expressed his regret for the "poisonous politics" that "allowed us to win the war." Publicly, in his massive six-volume history of World War II, written over the eight years following it and commonly known as his "memoirs," he consciously commandeered the story of the war: "History will be kind to me," he wrote wryly, "because I intend to write it."

As I looked into Churchill's memoirs and into the weighty tomes of British war historians to compare them with the archival records and eyewitness reports I was finding, I began to feel like that boy in Hans Christian Andersen's tale of the emperor's new clothes. Why had none of the major British historians, in their supposedly comprehensive overviews of the war, mentioned the Polish generals Anders and Maczek, and barely, if at all, General Sikorski, who was, after all, until his still-suspicious death in the plane crash in 1943, the leader of the Polish government in exile—Britain's first and, for a while, only fighting ally? Why, extraordinarily, had Churchill not mentioned Sikorski's death in his memoir entries for July 1943—or *at all* in his six-volume work? *Of course* the strains and complexities of the war demanded on-the-hoof compromises. *Of course* every country had its own war story, its own griefs and grievances; Poland didn't have a monopoly of suffering (although its death toll was second only to Russia's, and its people lost their country, as well).

Yet I began to see the blanks in Churchill's memoirs as a revealing negative image of his own no-go areas and of the new Cold War framework he was writing in: there was no mention of the decoding machine Enigma, or of the Bletchley Park intelligence unit that contributed as much as the military did to the defeat of the Nazis, none of the bad faith between him and Roosevelt at Tehran (which Stalin spotted at once, and exploited), and little about the role of the Red Army in winning the war. All of these touched more or less on Poland, that sensitive spot. Yet it was Churchill's record, backed with all the authority of his unique access to classified material, that set the tone for the view of the war for years afterwards, and still does. As British social historian J. H. Plumb wrote, thirty years after the outbreak of war, "We still move down the broad avenues which he drove through war's confusion and complexity." Churchill's road building was indeed remarkable for one man with such a heavy political weight on his shoulders. The only trouble was that his avenues buried the Poles under their tarmac.

In his fairy tale, Andersen describes the boy who tells the truth about the naked emperor as "a child who had no important job and could only see things as his eyes showed them to him." And it could be that good memoir is best written with "no important job"—like Rousseau, like Montaigne—in the sense of not being in hock to power or convention. It could be that the important, oxygenating task of memoir is to keep faith with the individual, the paradoxical, the unsystematic: the minute particulars of truth telling. Truth, said Francis Bacon famously, is the daughter of time, not of authority. (And even the matter of time disclosing the truth is, of course, questionable: distance from an event can take away as much as it gives.) The kind of memoir written with a political motive, or by ghostwriters, is different in kind from that led by the mind's eye and a real quest for truth—however partial and relative that truth will be, in the nature of things.

As Descartes, Montaigne, and Rousseau radically proposed long ago—and then demonstrated by bringing their ground-breaking "I" voices into literature—a felt relationship to the past can be as valuable, and often more trustworthy, than a rational, comprehensive one.

For myself, I'd found through talking with my father that I trusted contemporary eyewitness accounts most of all. I trusted what they saw with their eyes, at the time, on the ground. So I looked for more of them, to fill out what had happened before my father stepped into a picture he had no means of understanding. For Munich, I found an out-of-print memoir by Sydney Morrell, an English journalist who became my eyes and ears, and I brought in the accounts of writer Martha Gellhorn, who had, she said, "no qualifications except eyes and ears" (like the boy in the fairy tale; but what eyes and ears). For the Polish army's phenomenal, and still unsung, trek out of Siberia to the Western Front, I brought in General Anders's very felt personal memoir. Wherever I could, I wanted the "I" voice: the "I" witness. Like a bandleader bringing in soloists on kettle drums and saxophone, I brought in riffs—riffs of memoir.

And the last riff was my own: in 2001, sixty-two years after my father's escape from Soviet and Nazi occupation, I made a journey with a writer friend in Joe's footsteps, from Ukraine to his home village of Baligrod in the Carpathians. This eye-opening trek allowed me to feel underfoot the ground he'd covered, to see for myself the mountains, the beech forests, his straggly home village, and—still—the local people's residue of guardedness from the war, so like my father's own. It gave the narrative another foothold in the present, too, looping the time span of the story back like a lasso from current times.

And it allowed me to pick up a vital stitch from the past. By now it felt unthinkable to be writing about Poland, Germany, and World War II without mentioning the Holocaust, and yet it also seemed impossible to bring it in: my father wasn't Jewish, it wasn't part of his story, and it was too painful to touch on in passing, in a tipping-the-hat sort of way. But in Kraków one drizzly March morning, we stumbled across thousands of people in the main square, craning their necks to get a glimpse of a baseball-capped photographer on a high hoist in their midst. His name, people told us, was Ryszard Horowitz, and he was a well-known New York photographer here to take a picture of the scene for the forthcoming birthday of Pope John Paul II, who was born in the city. Back home, I emailed the photographer—only half expecting a response. His riveting reply told me that not only had he, too, been born in Kraków but he was the youngest survivor of Auschwitz, taken there at the age of three. Because memoir and travel writing are such agile forms, accommodating detour and discursive shifts ("I digress," says Sterne breezily in *Tristram Shandy*, "and I also progress, and both at the same time"), Ryszard's memories blended naturally into *Joe's War*, giving a child's-eye view—with humor, even—of the most twisted part of Hitler's war in that long-suffering part of Europe.

So the question of *who's got the story?* was woven right into the texture of the book for me, into its form—the plaited individual stories—and into its content. Who gets to tell the story of what goes on in a war? It's a question with a new slant now, with the soldiers blogging from the Iraq war. The ordinary foot soldier—unless a poet—has not, typically, told the history of a war. Nor have women, since we haven't been involved in combat until recently: the story hasn't been ours, though the fighting sons (and fathers and brothers) have been. As I read the history and heard Joe's story, I began to develop a mission to give my "ordinary Joe" father, and the eyewitnesses who had come my way, a voice against the shelf loads of books written about the tyrants who made their lives intolerable. Hitler's own turgid memoir, *Mein Kampf*, stands as an example of how badly written and distorted a memoir can be when it's bidding for power rather than truth.

But at a certain point, I knew I had to rein in that sense of mission: being up on a high horse is, after all, a bad position from which to write anything. For the most part, I jettisoned the crusade in favor of the memoir's limber form so that I could stay with the ambivalences, contradictions, and dead ends I was exploring, in myself as well as others. The occasional shaft of polemic or rhetoric could hit its mark quite well enough without turning the whole tome into a battlefield. And it wasn't a history book, either: I was tracking a figure—Joe—and my relationship to him, through a landscape of history. A landscape that just happened to be one of hot and cold wars.

Now, I see the book as part of an effervescence of time-lapsed stories from the monster-from-outside century. Often, like my father's, they've been bottled up during the Cold War, and now, unstoppered, they course into the current vogue for memoir. It's surely no accident that the memoir boom followed the dissolution of the Soviet Union: when the wall came down, people were let through, and the past was let through too. Its pent-up stories, with memoir at their core, have alchemized brilliantly into fiction and film. Jonathan Safran Foer's *Everything Is Illuminated,* Maria Lewycka's *A Short History of Tractors in Ukrainian,* the films *Goodbye Lenin* and *The Lives of Others,* all deal with the residue of massive tragedy in inventive and even playful ways, forging new forms so as not to get bogged down—precisely—in high-horsery, reprisals, and us-and-thems.

Perhaps memoir flourishes best in newly unfettered times, as it did in Enlightenment France, memoir's other heyday. For us in our times, it's been like awakening from a coma—the Cold War coma. Memoir sees the world anew, and its singular voice has often ended up—almost as a by-product—challenging received political, religious, or stylistic views: St. Augustine, Rousseau, Thoreau, Malcolm X. The misery memoirs of our own time may perhaps in their turn be challenging idealized notions of families. It seems we need periodically to remake orthodox narratives, particularly those forged out of power: to re-member the past—as Isis did literally with the scattered members of Osiris's celestial body—and bring it back to life. And we're once again in a time when orthodoxies need challenging by people trying to keep their eyes and minds open, to see, as the child did, the naked body of power as it struts the street. We need power and leaders, of course, not least to tell us a good story, but we don't need them to blinker or corral us into one overriding "vision." The province of memoir is simply to explore, free-range, some things that seem to need exploring and retrieving, wherever that leads.

The handmaiden of memoir in this task—the one who quietly hands us our cues and clues, if we attend to her—is, of course, memory. Something in the project of memory latches on to just the detail it needs (Proust's madeleine, the hammer) for its own purposes—which are what? Perhaps, as the aborigines and ancient Greeks thought, our stories really are, in some as yet inscrutable way, what we're here for; perhaps neuroscience or quantum physics will eventually fill us in on that. Meanwhile, it does seem that linking ourselves to what's around us, and to what went before, in however fragmentary and anecdotal a way, is necessary and satisfying, and possibly hardwired into us.

Joe's War has its own life now, as books do, and this essay is itself a version of *its* biography. The book has subtly changed my parents' and my lives and relationships: "by knowing her father's story, her own becomes that much richer," wrote the *New York Times*, which is true, and I'm glad to report that my father's pillow is hammer free. Things move on. My traveling companion in Ukraine—a lauded nature writer—died suddenly and too young last year; his latest book, just published posthumously, survives him. In it he writes of our joint trek across the Carpathian mountains in Joe's footsteps, seen through his own special interest of wood; a different version of exactly the same journey as in my book, but seen through another pair of eyes. As the central European saying has it, with an irony born of reverses of fortune and history, "There is nothing so unpredictable as the past." Or, as Milan Kundera wrote in one of his Cold War novels, "You think that just because it's already happened, the past is finished and unchangeable? Oh no, the past is cloaked in multi-coloured taffeta and every time we look at it we see a different hue." This is what I've found: the past is not dead and gone but can be changed; at worst, manipulated, at best, lit up from the inside, and breathed back to life.

Which reminds me, I must just go and check out the exact wording of the Official Secrets Act . . .

HELEN EPSTEIN

Coming to Memoir as a Journalist

. . .

WITH AN EXCERPT FROM
Where She Came From:
A Daughter's Search for Her Mother's History

FROM *Where She Came From:*
A Daughter's Search for Her Mother's History

During what had become years of haunting the library stacks, I had told the Czech librarian, Zuzana Nagy, parts of my grandmother's story and, like the three Jiřís, she had become something of a companion. Zuzana was born in Prague to survivor parents; I did not have to explain to her why I had no family papers. When I mentioned to her that I would love to know where in Prague Pepi might have lived when she returned, Zuzana frowned. Then she set off into the stacks and pulled out an elegantly bound volume titled *Adresář Královského města Prahy, 1910.*

The Prague telephone directory had a marbleized cover and thick white pages that were neither broken nor brown. I opened the book, looked under *W*, and gasped when I found *Josefa Weigertová, švadlena,* dressmaker. I stroked the cover, repeating my grandmother's address and telephone number of sixty years and a world earlier as if they were poetry:

Josefa Weigertová, švadlena
568-I Ovocný trh 17.

It was the first time I had ever seen her name in print. For a few minutes, I tried to think of a way of stealing the *Adresář.* Then I photocopied the page.

◆ ◆ ◆

Coming to Memoir as a Journalist

This is my starting point as a writer of memoir: In August 1968, I was a twenty-year-old American hitchhiking through Europe with friends. I started in Israel where I was a university student and flew to Athens. From Athens, we thumbed our way north toward Salonika, then traveled by train through what was then Yugoslavia to Vienna. Alone, I continued on to Prague, the city in which I was born after the end of World War II.

The Cold War was very much a fact that summer of 1968. People around the world were watching Czechoslovakia's experiment in "socialism with a human face" and wondering how long the Kremlin would allow it to continue. The Iron Curtain seemed permanent. Few westerners toured, let alone lived in, what was called Eastern Europe. Entry visas were required, applications were often rejected, and tourists had to register with the police wherever they traveled.

As my train left Vienna, then stopped in a no-man's-land between Austria and Czechoslovakia, I grew increasingly anxious. The border outside the train window was demarcated by watchtowers and barbed wire. The border guards were forbidding. I was carrying an American passport that identified Prague as my place of birth. There was always the possibility of a problem, and I was relieved when the train started moving again.

I had no conscious memories of Czechoslovakia—I had emigrated with my parents as a baby—but Czech was my first language and I grew up in the Czech refugee subculture of New York City. In that community, all the adults had fled either Nazism or Stalinism, two of the massive psychic traumas of the twentieth century.

The Nazis had dismembered the First Republic of Czechoslovakia—the only constitutional democracy in Central Europe at the time—and, in 1939, incorporated what is now the Czech Republic into the Third Reich, immediately arresting or killing thousands of anti-Nazi Czechs. Then, they targeted Czech Jews for extermination. Everyone in my immediate family except my parents was deported and murdered. My parents went through several concentration camps and returned to Prague as sole survivors of their families in 1945.

For three years, they and all of Czechoslovakia struggled to recover from Nazi occupation. Then, in February 1948, there was a Communist *putsch*. My father, a champion swimmer and member of the national Olympic committee, looked out his window at the armed demonstrators and determined to get his family out of the country immediately—in swimsuits, if necessary. He saw the Communists as "Nazis in different colored uniforms" and thought he would not be able to survive a second totalitarian regime. Luckily, he was able to obtain a visa for the United States. We arrived at New York's Idlewild Airport six months later.

When the train finally pulled into Prague's main railroad station on August 16, 1968, I was startled to hear our family language coming out of public loudspeakers, announcing arrivals and departures. Although I was a young adult, I spoke Czech like a five-year-old, a handicap that distorted my ability not only to speak but also to understand what was said to me. Strangers seemed like relatives. Even the black marketeers in the station seemed familiar. How could I refuse to exchange my dollars for *koruny* when the person asking seemed like a family intimate?

I wandered about Prague in a happy daze. I loved the stones and spires and colors and wondered if they had become encoded in my memory when I was being wheeled in my pram down the cobblestone streets. My hosts treated me like an heirloom and squabbled over where I would stay. I was to move from one doting family to another on August 21. Until then I was staying on the living room couch at an apartment on Veverkova Ulice or Squirrel's Street.

I hadn't paid attention to the news for weeks, not since I had landed in Greece, and so was unprepared when, that morning at five, my hosts woke me with the words *Jsme obsazene*—"We're occupied." I remember saying that was okay with me, that I'd manage to get to my next host family by myself if they had things to do. Then I tuned into the strange crunching noise outside and understood they were talking about *military* occupation.

I heard three kinds of noise: the crunch of tanks on cobblestones, the droning of planes, the *rat-tat-tat* of shooting in the park nearby. I couldn't call home, as international phone lines had been cut. My hosts left to stock up on food and gasoline. I got dressed and went outside. A line of armored tanks rolled toward me.

I'm not sure when I began to dissociate what I saw from what I felt. I stood frozen in place, taking in like a camera the machine guns on the tanks, the Russian soldiers crouched behind them, the grim spectators, and the cyclists who had attached Czech flags to their motorbikes. I remember wondering whether that was a heroic or suicidal act. I remember a wall drawing that a graffiti artist had scrawled in chalk: the vulva-shaped outline of Czechoslovakia with a Russian sickle piercing its center.

I know that, after a few minutes, my knees turned to Jell-O, like the knees of an animated cartoon character. I hurried back inside, turned the radio on, found a typewriter, and began recording what I saw and heard.

Although I did not yet think of myself as a writer, I had already developed a writing habit. It began during mandatory "rest periods" of summer camp, sending reports to parents and friends about what I was doing and how I felt about it. In those regular bulletins from the wild, I discovered the satisfactions of putting words to feelings that were exciting or joyful or painful and revising those words until my feelings made sense to me. I loved all the rituals of writing: clearing physical and mental space, setting aside a silent time, choosing my materials, watching with elation as ideas I didn't know I had filled up the blank page.

I had often seen the power of letters dramatized in paintings or at the theater or opera. The heroine stands at center stage or sits at a desk near a window, holding an envelope in her hands, gazing at it as though it holds something magical. If she is an actress or a singer, she passionately gives voice to her love, bitterness, disappointment, anger, regret. It has always been easier for me to write about what I feel deeply than to say it.

On August 21, 1968, alone in the apartment on Squirrel's Street, I wrote about how it felt to be twenty years old, terrified, and stuck in the middle of the Soviet invasion of Czechoslovakia. Focusing on the words clacking out of the old typewriter relegated my physical reality to the background and provided a measure of control. It gave me a sense of agency at a time when I was helpless. It was an antidote to passivity. Like those actresses and opera singers, I sent a letter to the world.

Two days later, I was evacuated from Prague to Paris on a special train for foreigners. I mailed what I had written to two newspapers: the *New York Times* and the *Jerusalem Post*. The *Post* published it as an eyewitness account of the invasion.

Forty years later, I can see how my private experience in the context of public space set me on the road toward writing memoir. I'm still uncovering new layers of sequelae in my experience of the Soviet invasion. Like many memoirists, I've discovered that my particular location at the intersection of personal and collective experience, with roots back in early childhood, has provided me with an inexhaustible subject.

Writers come to memoir from many different literary forms. Some are poets, bringing with them a lyric voice and new language. Some are novelists, skilled in characterization and narrative drive. Some are essayists, masters of introspection and the elaboration of ideas. Some are travel writers whose adventures allow us to voyage vicariously. A growing number are extraliterary professionals—physicians, psychoanalysts, academics, business and sports celebrities—joining the aristocrats, elder statesmen, and military officers who traditionally wrote memoirs at the end of their lives.

I came to memoir from journalism. After I returned to university in Israel in the fall of 1968, the *Jerusalem Post* offered me a part-time job as a reporter. I wrote feature stories, short narratives about interesting people and situations, and decided to go to journalism school.

Traditional third-person journalism as taught in 1970 at Columbia University was the antithesis of memoir. We were drilled to focus our eyes and ears *out* onto public space and to eradicate personal opinion. Emotion had no place in our discipline, either; neutral accuracy was our goal. We were to approach a subject without prejudice or preconception and record reality as precisely as we could. Imagining or embellishing the truth, let alone *making things up*, was the province of creative writing programs. I recall a certain high moral tone on this point among my teachers. We journalists did not traffic in useless, self-indulgent fantasy. We did research, made acute observations, investigated records, asked probing questions, got the facts.

After this proactive work, in the writing itself, we were to erase all trace of ourselves. I liked that idea. Since childhood, I had been fascinated by the properties of invisible ink, and here was a chance to be there and then not be there, to become invisible.

The ideal of objectivity was still largely unchallenged by postmodernist ideas in 1970. It sufficed to assess the "truthfulness" and "reliability" of two independent sources to verify a fact, to record it accurately and in context; then check and double-check. My teachers edited my work for concision as well as readability. They questioned my descriptions and characterizations and stamped out feelings or opinions as though they were weeds. Although third-person journalism prized a reporter's "eye for detail" and an "ear for the telling quote," it eliminated all evidence of the human being who possessed these sensory organs.

I started writing freelance for the Sunday *New York Times* cultural pages soon after graduation and became a journalism professor at New York University. I taught my students what I had been taught: the who, what, where, when, and why of a story; the suppression of their own voices, feelings, and opinions; the ideal of themselves as sponges—absorbing, recording, assembling it all into a coherent narrative, pyramid structure, most important facts up top. I taught them how to tell a story without expressing editorial opinion. I urged them to see their role as invisible conduits between subject and reader, and of course to work on deadline within strict word limits. I drilled them in terseness, concision, accuracy.

But I couldn't remain impervious to the counterculture and new political movements of the 1960s. The activist media were loudly challenging the status quo and leading me to think very differently about writing. I realized that the objective journalism I had so idealistically and naïvely embraced was in fact riddled with prejudice about what was fit to print.

Like many New Yorkers, I grew up thinking that if something wasn't reported in the *Times,* it hadn't happened. Now I realized how much wasn't reported in its pages. As I witnessed how editors developed and assigned articles, I saw how simplistic and exclusionary my education had been. It wasn't only that traditional journalism, like most American professions, was permeated by political, racial, social, age, and gender biases that shaped the definition of newsworthiness. Or that media, like all institutions, have their own cultural norms. Or that money and power and tradition determined access to news coverage. I realized that importance was determined inside a rarified private space by editors who did not venture much out into the public world.

I had grown accustomed to writing on assignment, that is, pitching story ideas to editors for consideration and more often taking their direction about what was or was not deemed fit to print. In the 1970s, my *Times* editors were almost all men. I learned to speak their language, filled with military and sports metaphors. I wrote not in my own voice but in a more formal way, hewing to the institutional guidelines. All sources, for example, were to be identified by their honorifics or as "Mr." or "Mrs." No four-letter words. In describing student conductors at Tanglewood, I could not report that some of their faces were so transfigured by the music that they looked like they were having orgasms. "Not fit to print" in the *Times.*

When I worked for women's magazines, there was a different vocabulary to learn and a different kind of censorship. Advertisers and their products were not to be criticized. *Cosmopolitan* even gave its writers a style book, instructing them on taboo words as well as favored punctuation.*

I began to question the role of traditional journalistic criteria, to pay attention to what was going on between me and my interviewee during interviews, to refuse deadlines, to take my time, to choose my

* For a minimemoir on my experience at the magazine, see "That Cosmopolitan Writer" in *MORE: A Journalism Review* (October 1973): 13; also available at www.helenepstein.com.

subjects and their scope by my own criteria of importance. I continued to write about people that the *New York Times* deemed important—celebrated musicians such as Leonard Bernstein or Yo-Yo Ma or theatrical producer Joe Papp, whose biography I eventually wrote. But I also tried to pitch obscure people or people who didn't employ press agents, like the late violin teacher Dorothy DeLay, who had not yet been the subject of a profile.

I knew I wasn't neutral in my choice of subject. I was simply becoming more interested in writing about people like myself: women, immigrants, people who had a history of trauma. I was becoming aware that we all perceive events—public and private—through the double prism of our culture and personal experience, and it resonates in multiple echo chambers of memory. Unlike journalism, which demands that reporters ignore or subsume that subjective reality, memoir encourages writers to plumb it.

In 1976, I tried to persuade my editors at the *Times Magazine* to assign me an article about sons and daughters of Holocaust survivors—a then-unrecognized group that had, as my editor put it, "no press agent, no organizational letterhead, and no expert vouching for their existence." I argued that I, myself, was the daughter of concentration camp survivors and that there were probably a quarter of a million other people like me. But my pitch was ignored until Stanford University's Medical School issued a press release about an Israeli psychiatrist studying the effects of the Holocaust on the second generation, and *Time* printed some of it, thereby validating my subject as news.

In 1976, the *Times Magazine* finally assigned me to write about the group now known as "children of survivors" who were "possessed by a history they had never lived." I identified myself briefly as one but, in my piece, focused on my interviewees. The article provoked over five hundred letters—lengthy, intimate, full of provocative material—that made it clear I had a book on my hands.

Although it was easy to get a publisher, it was hard to jettison years of training, turn my investigative skills on myself, and transform a magazine article into the memoir *Children of the Holocaust.* The terms "survivor" and "Holocaust" were not yet household words; the idea of the Soup Nazi unimaginable. I found it very difficult to sustain the belief that my subject was important and that my private experience could be considered significant in the public sphere. Neither my friends nor my family were enthusiastic about my project. But, feeling a compulsion to write it, I turned away from third-person journalism and began my book like this:

> For years it lay in an iron box buried so deep inside me that I was never sure just what it was. I knew I carried slippery combustible things more secret than sex and more dangerous than any shadow or ghost. Ghosts had shape and name. What lay inside my iron box had none. Whatever lived inside me was so potent that words crumbled before they could describe.

Children of the Holocaust is partly a work of reportage that lays out the 5ws up front and includes extensive research and in-depth interviews. It is an examination of the consequences of growing up in a family whose members have been murdered, whose community and culture have been eradicated, where parents struggle with all the many manifestations of what psychologists now call post-traumatic stress disorder.

I structured it like challah, braiding my personal narrative, oral history, and reportage, because the concept of intergenerational psychic trauma was then new, and as a journalist breaking new ground, I felt obliged to produce more persuasive evidence than my own experience.

Children of the Holocaust was translated into several languages, helped create an international second-generation community, is viewed by mental health professionals as a contribution to the study of trauma, and has stayed in print for nearly thirty years. Like many memoirs that strike a collective chord, it served a crucial healing function not only for myself but for many others—children of immigrants; children of other genocide survivors; children of parents traumatized by war, loss, and abuse. I like to think of my first book as a contribution to what Jews call *tikkun olam*, or "repair of the world." In one of his essays, V. S. Naipaul writes: "However creatively one travels, however deep an experience in childhood or middle-age, it takes thought (a sifting of impulses, ideas, and references that become more multifarious as one grows older) to understand what one has lived through or where one has been."*

That process of making meaning is very similar to the process of piecing together other kinds of narrative, whether in psychoanalysis or fiction. What distinguishes memoir from these other two endeavors is its attempt to produce a finished work that elucidates memory and its workings, separates it from fantasy as far as possible, and renders lived rather than imagined experience.

Within the literary world, I've encountered a kind of disdain for memoir that my journalism professors expressed for creative writing. *How lazy memoirists are!* novelists exclaim, as though it were easier to adhere to facts in constructing a story than to invent a fictional world. *And this healing stuff. What a nonliterary pollutant to bring into what should be a purely artistic activity!*

As someone whose family history is frequently termed a "fiction" or a "hoax" by Holocaust revisionists from Canada to Iran, I'm particularly committed to the memoir form. In addition to its unique literary qualities, it serves a crucial historical role. As the poet Czesław Miłosz, another survivor of the European totalitarianisms, writes: "Unless we can relate it to ourselves personally, history will always be more or less of an abstraction. . . . Doubtless every family archive that perishes, every account book that is burnt, every effacement of the past reinforces classifications and ideas at the expense of reality."†

* * *

* *Finding the Center* (London: André Deutsch, 1984), 12.
† *Native Realm: A Search for Self-Definition* (Berkeley and Los Angeles: University of California Press, 1981), 20.

In addition to exterminating human beings, the Nazis destroyed family and community history throughout most of Central and Eastern Europe. My next book, the memoir *Where She Came From: A Daughter's Search for Her Mother's History,* was written with the idea of reconstructing that history. I began working on it as a way of mourning my mother's sudden death in 1989. My work was made infinitely easier by Czechoslovakia's Velvet Revolution that fall and the subsequent opening up of archives and museums. Working from my mother's unpublished interviews and memoir, I was able to trace and document my maternal ancestors back to the beginning of the nineteenth century and to write about the kind of lives they led. I was particularly interested in my maternal grandmother, Pepi, whose absence I felt keenly as a little girl. But I also wanted to find out as much as I could about the world she had come from before the Nazis and the Communists erased it. I wanted to reconstruct a time, as my colleague Charlie Fenyvesi titled one of his memoirs of pre-Holocaust Hungary, "when the world was whole."

In writing *Where She Came From,* I not only traveled through Central Europe but also cruised the stacks of research libraries and wandered into such esoteric academic subspecialties as the history of the production of alcoholic spirits and the sociology of the first generation of Viennese psychoanalysts. I searched through dusty ledgers, sat in old cemeteries in the Czech-Moravian highlands, and read other people's memoirs, starting with what scholars identify as the first one by a Jewish woman—seventeenth-century merchant Gluckl of Hameln—right through twentieth-century memoirs by women such as Heda Kovaly, whose book *Under a Cruel Star* is crucial for anyone trying to grasp the sequential blows of Nazism and Stalinism.

In reading them, I paid attention not only to the facts but to what they evoked in my own mind and heart. I tried to find—as French writer Marie Cardinal titled one of her memoirs—*les mots pour le dire,* or my own "words to say it." I learned to follow wherever the road led—irrespective of unlikely destinations. I learned to capitalize on, rather than minimize, drama, to trust my subjectivity, to let myself get lost in free association and introspection. I continued to struggle with the most difficult thing for a writer coming to memoir from journalism: making the claim that my subject was important or, as the newspaper I used to write for put it, "fit to print."

Women writers and writers from minority groups have struggled with this problem for a long time, and while literary culture has grown steadily more inclusive of differences of all kinds, it is still a challenge, particularly in a market-driven publishing environment. Memoirs by writers like Eva Hoffman, Jung Chang, Patricia Hampl, Jan Morris, and Kay Redfield Jamison that have stubbornly staked out their own idiosyncratic territory have inspired me to explore mine and to believe in its importance and validity.

For the past seven years, I've been digging into the intimate subject of first love. Like everything else I've written, *First Love* is part biography, part cultural history, as well as first-person narrative based on memory. It engages questions of sexual and emotional development against a backdrop of history and culture; it explores an adolescence in the 1960s.

My first love came from a traumatic background of his own: he was the son of blacklisted American Communists, people for whom my parents did not have much sympathy. These larger events in both of our families colored and provided a counterpoint to our relationship. He had been an old friend, and I called him when I got home, that August of 1968; our personal history is linked in my mind with the Russian invasion of Czechoslovakia. Forty years later, I am still mining the material at that intersection of public and private space.

JUNE CROSS

All in the Family

• • •

WITH AN EXCERPT FROM
Secret Daughter:
A Mixed-Race Daughter and the Mother Who Gave Her Away

FROM *Secret Daughter:*
A Mixed-Race Daughter and the Mother Who Gave Her Away

"Mommie! Mommie!" I called out, wanting to show her something. "Come see!"

She ignored me, finished her conversation, and put down the pot she was working with. She wiped her hands on the half apron she wore over her little black dress. Then she took me by the hand and led me toward the bathroom.

I tried to pull her the other way.

"But, Mommie, I wanted to show you something!"

She quickly and quietly closed the door and sat down on the toilet lid so that we were face-to-face. "Didn't I tell you to call me 'Aunt Norma'?"

I giggled and put my hand over my mouth. I had totally forgotten about our little game.

"This isn't funny!" she hissed.

"I'm sorry, Aunt Mommie—I mean, Aunt Norma," I said, giggling even harder, thinking of the time she and I had giggled ourselves silly while Uncle Paul was trying to say grace. But now, looking into her eyes, I stopped and caught my breath.

I nearly didn't recognize her. Her narrow eyes looked like an evil witch's.

"June, this is very serious!" she said, her voice as sharp as razors. "Larry could lose his job. We could all end up homeless! You won't be able to stay with Peggy and Paul in Atlantic City! Our future depends on this! Do you understand me?"

I tried to back away, but I bumped up against the clothes hamper. Trapped between the toilet and the wall, I responded with a mask of my own—my small voice.

"Yes, Aunt Norma."

When the party was over, after everyone had left, my mother sat down by the side of the bed and apologized for being so harsh.

"I'm sorry I yelled at you," she said, "but this may determine Larry's entire future. This agent could be very important for Larry, to help him get jobs. I didn't want him thinking I'd already been married and had children; it might not reflect well on Larry."

When Mom finally married Larry, his family disowned him. I thought I was the reason—that my failure to remember the rules of the game at that party had made his family mad.

Over the years Mom and Larry developed two circles of friends: those who knew about me and those who didn't. Gradually my visits began to coincide with those occasions when it was convenient for me to be seen.

◆ ◆ ◆

All in the Family

Few conversations in America get complicated as quickly as those involving race and family. In the fifties, few subjects were more taboo than unmarried women having children. Miscegenation and illegitimacy, shame and guilt—these emotions form the contours of my life story.

I am the African American child of a white woman and a black man. My parents were never married. I was raised never knowing this truth. I didn't even know how my parents had met. I knew my biological father's name, James "Stump" Cross, but aside from the fact that he was African American and involved in show business, I could have told you little about him. I was certain—or fairly certain—that my white mother, Norma Booth, who I thought was part Blackfoot Indian (wrong), had been deserted by my father when I was two (wrong) and married my stepfather, who I thought was a Russian Jew (right).

I also knew that Aunt Peggy and Uncle Paul, who had raised me in the black neighborhood of Atlantic City, were not really my aunt and uncle. So as I considered writing a memoir, I faced questions of accuracy, authenticity, honesty, and some pretty searing emotions.

What I knew about my own history was what the lens of my memory had recorded. And most of that was shrouded in secrecy. I didn't *have* a secret, I *was* the secret. My mother often hid the fact that she had given birth to a black man's child. That's why at age five she sent me to live with "Aunt Peggy" and "Uncle Paul."

My biggest struggle in writing *Secret Daughter*, therefore, was not with the content of the story but with how to describe my journey to unravel the secrets. How much history did one need to know in order to understand the motivations of my parents? In order to understand how external events had affected my life?

Linear stories are easier for people to follow, but my story—and my understanding of my own story—didn't unfold so neatly. How does one articulate the *absence* of history, and the meaning of that absence to a life? I had never met my grandparents and knew nothing about them—not even their names. I never understood what my white mother's ethnic background was or what she did for a living. I didn't even know my father's whole name until I was seven or eight. I didn't learn what he actually did for a living until I was twenty. In an early draft of my memoir, I wrote that, when my mother first introduced me to my father, around the time I was five or six, I didn't know what a "father" was. My editor couldn't understand the sentence, and I couldn't figure out how to explain it. I could have said my father was a stranger to me, but that wouldn't have begun to describe the unrecognized and unacknowledged void that I carried within me.

Had I told the story the way it actually happened, the way my own diaries, photographs, and memories remember it, the first two-thirds of *Secret Daughter* would have been filled with my recollections of happy days—my life as a black middle-class child who went to dance classes and summer camp, who taught Sunday school and played piano during talent competitions, and who dreamed of being Miss America.

But *story* requires tension and surprise, my editor kept reminding me. Yet I did not begin my life as a "secret daughter." I was, simply, my mother's daughter. The necessity for concealing my true identity was apparent to some adults around me, but never spoken of to me. Those who cared for me made every effort to shelter me from this fiction.

The moment when I came to full awareness, readers tell me, forms one of the most heartbreaking sections of my book, although I don't remember feeling heartbreak as a child. I was four or five when my mother scolded me for calling her "Mommie" in public. I was forced to hold several competing notions in my mind at the same time—that my mother was my mother yet not my mother, that something about us was dangerous enough to destroy us, that the world was not a safe place in ways far more threatening than what could happen if I crossed the street against the light. I remember parts of the encounter more vividly than I remember what I did this morning after breakfast—the feel of the small white tiles on the bathroom floor against my feet, the white aluminum clothes hamper chilly behind my back, the fierceness in her eyes, angry. Was she actually angry at me, like an "evil witch," as I wrote about it in the book? Or was she a lioness protecting her cub? Or was that fear I saw? How can I know for sure, from a distance of nearly fifty years? In my child's memory the story is filed next to the fairy tales about Hansel and Gretel and Little Red Riding Hood, but did I know the meaning of those frightening tales at that young age?

Writing *Secret Daughter* began as a way of correcting the public record. The false story that my white mother and stepfather adopted me needed to be replaced by the truth. Telling the secret, making it public, was my way of inserting my story into the national story. I was motivated not by a desire to tell the story of a fascinating life but because I know, as a student of racial history and race relations in America, that my story has been replicated untold millions of times by sons and daughters who never found their way to a book publisher. In order to tell my story, though, I had to use the tools of the documentary filmmaker, the medium in which I'm most fluent, as well as the sources of the historian. Here is where I encountered the crevasse between history and documentary, between the oral tradition and the public record.

For documentary filmmakers, the editing room becomes a studio where we shape and weave bits of image and sound to arrive at an emotional truth based on the best research we can muster. Beginning documentarians are normally taught to follow the timeline of their shooting, fashioning from the ribbons of tape a chronological tale that emphasizes a what-came-first, what-came-next scenario. This is a what-happened approach to storytelling. It works well if one accepts at face value what one sees, without considering the history and the backstory of the participants and their communities. But fledgling documentarians inevitably falter trying to introduce public history into their personal stories. If one puts history where it belongs—before the events that unfolded in front of the camera— it usually leads to dull filmmaking. The question one faces is, How much history do you *need* to know? The answer, in documentary, is, Only what you need in order to understand what's going on.

In other words, the documentarian's approach to filmmaking emphasizes externalities—it favors what the eye can see or what the ear can hear. As a student of the form back in the seventies, I felt its tyrannical nature. The very first film I ever did, seven minutes long, was a rumination on the nature of time. I was a maudlin twenty-one-year-old, and for some reason a recording of Nina Simone introducing her rendition of "Who Knows Where the Time Goes?" at the New York Philharmonic on October 26, 1969, caught my attention. "What is this thing called time?" Simone pondered. "You go to work by the clock. You get your martini in the afternoon by the clock. You drink your coffee by the clock. You have to get on the plane at a certain time—and it goes on and on and on." I saw, as Simone did, that "time is a dictator."

Probably because I was already mulling over how to present the narrative sequence of my own life, time became the first mystery of

personal storytelling for me. I needed to become a historian. I had
to search through a wealth of documents for the written record and
the artifacts of important moments. I had to listen to the meanings
carried in oral histories. This historical digging yielded a more
detailed framing of what happened to me and my parents. But as
I researched my own life history for the documentary that ultimately
became *Secret Daughter*, I discovered that historical records themselves are fallible and incomplete.

I grew up in a black section of Atlantic City, before the civil rights
movement. We had, within one block of my house, two grocery stores,
two barbershops, a tailor, a notary public, and a bookie. But aside
from the title deeds in the city hall, there is no information on the
people who owned those homes and lived in that community. There's
no film of them for the simple reason that those who owned cameras
and film in those days saw no reason to document the lives of the
black community. It was as if we did not exist.

Each person's unique story helps to fill in that void. But the telling
is not simple. As a writer of memoir working in the smaller yet deeper
dimension of feelings, flow, and structure—*my own interior history*—
I struggled often with which bits of my life I would choose and how
I would explain them.

Personal memories spring from the imagined and real connections among places, people, and things. This is where history and
memoir diverge. Textbook history is arrived at by consensus, dulled
at the edges. It is drawn from careful inspection of documents and
limited by the records one can find. The grand sweep of history feels
linear, even though it is messy and fraught with competing ideas and
conflicting circles of influence. But for the memoirist, history and
memory conflate to form a story we want to tell about ourselves,
and that narrative arc changes as we grow older, as the world turns.

So how is one to bring together the fragments of inaccurate or incomplete history and faulty or incomplete memory? This is where
the detective work begins. Finding information on my father's family posed the greatest challenge. He had been a song and dance man

with a promising career back in the thirties and forties. There are those who say that if you've seen a Jerry Lewis comedy, you can imagine my father's career—my dad was a more nimble, and frankly more talented, version of Lewis. Since I never saw my father perform, I had to rely on movies and homemade films to see this.

As I went back into the census data to trace the lineage of my father, an African American man, I had to rely on the notes of faceless government bureaucrats with bad handwriting. Was my grandmother's name Wilkes or Wilkinson or Wilson? It depended on whether I looked at my father's birth certificate, my grandmother's marriage certificate, or *her* birth certificate.

As I went further back, things got tougher. During the nineteenth century, black women were often referred to by first names only—so one is left to deduce from the person's age and occupation and the names of her children whether the Caroline you're looking at in Philadelphia in 1910 may be the same Caroline who owned two hundred acres of land in southern Virginia in 1890. And in antebellum records, even the names of the female slaves are lost. We were just breeders, after all.

Since I never met my grandparents, I had to search birth and death certificates to find their names: Rosalee Wilkes and Purcell Cross, although their names were spelled differently in different places. Was it "Rosilie" or "Rose Lee" or "Rosalee"? Was it "Percival" or "Purcell"? My grandmother was described as a domestic on her wedding license, and my father's friends say she left Percy when her two children were young. After that she worked and lived in rich people's homes, leaving her two children to raise themselves. At the end of her life, she ran a speakeasy.

My relatives remembered that she lived somewhere in North Philadelphia, but they couldn't remember exactly where. Using estate and title records, I finally found the house my father had bought for her—a wide three-floor, four-bedroom row house with parquet floors that had been left to deteriorate. It took me three days of door knocking in the neighborhood where she had once lived to find the woman I was told had been her best friend. In our interview, I discovered that she and my grandmother had lived in a committed relationship, as partners, for almost twenty-five years. My grandmother, in other words, was a lesbian.

Within my extended family, I ran into the disconnect between the oral tradition and the written record. The oral tradition, as passed down from generation to generation, was that a servant girl named Jane had worked in the residence of Supreme Court Justice Roger Taney, and that a "prince from Madagascar," walking by the house one day, had seen her, paid a price for her, married her, and been disowned from his Madagascar family forever.

Judge Taney was a powerful man. It should be easy to document this. However, his meticulously kept personal records make no mention of either a slave or a servant by the name of Jane. In fact, women were not named in those days—they were simply "females" with an age given. Judge Taney's father had a female slave who matched the age Jane would have been, but she was given to Judge Taney's brother, Robert, as part of the estate, and her presence is recorded there long after our Jane should have been married and bearing children.

Even on my mother's side, the Anglo-European side that is better documented, I ran into problems. A cousin had told me that I was related to Miles Standish. My immediate reaction was, "But I don't want to be related to Miles Standish." It turned out I wasn't. My mother's ancestral tree, very well documented thanks to Mormon genealogical research, did indeed go back to colonial Boston. I was related to a ship's captain named William Pearce (or Pierse, or Pierce) who plied the waters between London, Boston, and the Bahamas in a ship called the *Lyon* and who had made as many as thirty crossings during his career. Pearce also compiled the first almanac published in North America in 1639, for Harvard College. My mother's plutocratic roots went deeper than anyone knew.

Pearce was a person with standing, a person with a documented life. But what about those unnamed huddled masses who were illiterate, whose stories are lost? I know their names—the one who

fought in the Revolutionary War, received a shoulder injury and filed
for disability; the one who joined the Mormons and survived the
Mountain Meadows massacre—but I know nothing else. So I am
forced to read the documented history, imagine their lives, and follow the trail of the ancestors with standing.

Captain William Pearce had a dark side—he kidnapped Indians
from New England and sold them into slavery in Spain. He brought
one of the first African slaves to Jamestown, Virginia, in 1639. She
was a woman listed on the ship's manifest only as "Angela." For all
I know, she was one of my father's ancestors.

I found a rather eerie footnote in Captain Pearce's life story: he
had three wives during his lifetime. And the first, who came to
Jamestown on a ship back in 1639 with that slave named Angela, was
named June.

She died at Jamestown, and left no memoir to tell her tale.

So here I am, the descendent of a slave trader and a slave. Where
does this leave my relationship to history in a country where you are
either one of the conquerors or one of the oppressed? And how do
I reconcile these internal and external versions of that history when
the two can be so at odds? You could say I walk a tightrope between
the two. But having researched the stories and histories of so many
like me, so many others on my mother's side who both supported
and fought against slavery—and on my father's side who used their
relationship with whites to move forward, socially—it's hard to
claim that I am the only one like me. The more I learned about my
story, the less peculiar it seemed.

By the time I had traced the census back to the mid-nineteenth century, I found eighteen thousand souls in the United States with whom
I could claim some kind of relationship. They are cousins four or five
times removed. That moves my understanding of memoir and history
beyond documentary, past the personal, into the archetypal. It's impossible to feel like a lone soul surrounded by those kinds of numbers.

I recently reread Virginia Woolf's "A Sketch of the Past," in which she distinguishes between "moments of nonbeing" and "moments of being." Moments of nonbeing are what most of us experience in our day-to-day lives—we get out of bed, brush our teeth, eat breakfast, walk to the subway. It's as if we live behind a veil of cotton wool or, to use a more culturally specific metaphor, as if we exist only behind the curtain of sound supplied by our iPods.

But then every so often, by serendipity or happenstance, something shifts. You have a conversation with a stranger whose story of hard luck and triumph speaks louder than any other. You walk out of your house and catch the scent of Jamaican jerk chicken being cooked the same moment you notice a band of smoke forming a black ribbon across a cerulean blue sky on a particularly bloody Tuesday one September. You enter a dingy room and your eyes meet those of the person you will marry, and you remember the exact tinge of yellow in the fading Christmas lights and the slight tilt of the ripped red and white linoleum floor as you walked to a barstool, with the smooth texture of the wooden chair polished by many hands, and how his palms were warm with sweat and cold from the bottle of beer he had been holding just before he extended his hand. In these moments, undocumented and unknowable to the historian, time slows and it seems you've joined the master current of the universe, as if your puny existence merged, in an instant, with human history that unites us all.

This is the role of memoir—a form more impressionistic and personal than autobiography, more introspective and less rigorous than historical narrative. The current surge of interest in this genre begins as an affirmation that the hegemonic "great man" theory of history ignores the stories of the bookie and the barbershop owners and those who shopped at the grocery stores in my Atlantic City neighborhood. It asserts that we all have our stories to tell and that those stories are as individual as wildflowers. I suspect, and I certainly believe, that by writing our own lives, we join the beauty of the field.

MICHAEL PATRICK MACDONALD

It's All in the Past

. . .

WITH AN EXCERPT FROM
Easter Rising: A Memoir of Roots and Rebellion

FROM *Easter Rising: A Memoir of Roots and Rebellion*

The therapist watched me as I tried to answer her question, only her third in what seemed like small talk to get acquainted.

Shit, here we go again, I thought.

All my life I had struggled with the answer to the question "How many are in your family?" and it wasn't getting any easier. My mother had lost the baby, Patrick, a year before I was born, but we always included him in the count, since we thought of him as a kind of guardian sibling. As a child, sometime I would say, "Eleven, but one died." People would ask, shocked, "*Eleven* brothers and sisters?" I was proud to be from such a big family. . . .

After Davey died I started saying, "Eleven, but two died." But then people exclaimed, "Oh my God!" and wanted to know how the two had died. Once I saw how people recoiled at the mention of someone jumping off a roof, I usually didn't feel like talking about it. I learned to say, "Nine," relieved to have to deal only with an "Irish Catholics" comment. But I felt guilty about cutting Davey out of the count, even though I no longer cared about childish birth-rate contests. I started including both Davey and Patrick again.

But now, with Frankie and Kevin dead and only seven of us remaining alive, I had answered a few times, "Eleven, but four died," only to see the person look horrified, not wanting to ask how. Then, to comfort them, I'd explain that it wasn't that bad, that I only knew three of them, that Patrick was a baby who'd died before I was born. Which only made their faces contort more. I had to do some quick math in my head before answering at all, since Kathy was now permanently brain damaged and increasingly schizophrenic. She talked to herself all day and wrote childhood rhymes on any paper she could find, an existence that seemed somewhere between life and death. I felt more like I was one of six, not seven, survivors, and that brought me back to thinking, *Who's next?* Then I'd want to call home to make sure everyone was okay or wonder whether the strange feeling in my throat was cancer.

I'd only paused for a few seconds before giving my "eleven, but four died" version, but the therapist looked confused. She straightened up in her chair to pursue the question further.

"How did they die?" she asked straightforwardly. I was glad she wasn't asking with the wide eyes that usually accompanied the question. Anytime Ma had to answer the question, she said they were in a car accident. I guessed she wanted to keep it simple, rather than getting into suicide, jumps and falls from rooftops, bank robberies, and prison deaths....

Okay, here goes, I thought. *Remember Patrick even though you never met him. And keep Kathy off the list of the dead.*

◆ ◆ ◆

It's All in the Past

My friend's seventy-year-old aunt lit into him on Broadway in South Boston after she heard his name was listed in the acknowledgments of my first memoir, *All Souls.*

"What did I do?" he pleaded as she crossed the street and came at him, her finger pointed.

"You're in that goddamn book!" she screamed. "And that book is all lies!"

"Did you read it?" he asked her, surprised, since it had only just been published.

"No!" she bellowed. "And I'm not going to read it, either!"

My friend ran to the other side of a parked car, establishing a safe distance before asking, "Why not?" He expected he was dealing with Southie's entrenched code of silence, a legacy of our neighborhood's drug don, James "Whitey" Bulger, who had controlled the town through years of murder, bank robberies, and overdoses.

"I lived in that housing project for thirty years," she shrieked, "and we never had cockroaches!"

The denial was so deep in our neighborhood that we didn't even want to acknowledge the bugs. Never mind that Southie had the highest concentration of white poverty in America.* Never mind that the town was controlled by Irish mob boss Whitey Bulger, finally exposed in 1999 as a protected FBI informant. Never mind that local politicians looked the other way as gangsters flooded our neighborhood with angel dust, cocaine, and crack, leaving a trail of dead young people.

Even today—a decade after Whitey Bulger went on the lam, tipped off by his FBI handlers about impending indictments—Southie has the city's highest rate of overdose from heroin and other painkillers.

Never mind that. Forget about it. It's all in the past. These are the mantras we grew up with in Southie.

Or even worse: "It never happened."

I had a book contract when I wrote *All Souls*, but I didn't think I was writing a story anyone would read, beyond a few loyal friends. I was therefore able to write freely about my experiences growing up in a world where the truth had always been suppressed. I was the ninth of eleven children. Four of us were lost to the effects of poverty. A baby, Patrick, died of pneumonia after being denied admission to the hospital in 1964, before Medicaid, when hospitals weren't required to admit welfare babies with no insurance. In 1979, when I was thirteen, I saw my brother Davey, ten years older, lying in the street in front of our apartment after he jumped off a project rooftop. (Among its many off-the-charts statistics, Southie has long held the city's highest suicide rate.) When I was eighteen, my brother Frank, a New England Golden Gloves boxing champion, was killed while robbing a Wells Fargo armored bank truck. And eight months later my brother Kevin was found hanging in prison under suspicious circumstances.

And there were other tragedies. My sister Kathy went off another project rooftop after a fight over pills when I was fourteen; she lay in a coma for four months and is now partially paralyzed with serious brain damage. A year later, my mother received a minor wound from

* *U.S. News and World Report*, October 9, 1994.

a stray bullet as I stood next to her while she washed dishes. In 1991, my thirteen-year-old younger brother Steven was convicted of manslaughter when his best friend died while playing with a gun; two years later a state appeals court unanimously overturned his unjust conviction.

It took me a while to see it, but South Boston, often described as insular, was psychologically as well as geographically so. The neighborhood sits on a peninsula. Downtown Boston is only accessible by two bridges. If Southie's borders weren't enough fortification from the outside world, the Old Colony project where my family lived was an even more closed world, a subculture within a subculture. While South Boston's politicians often presented the myth of the hardscrabble yet blue-collar neighborhood ("blue collar" being the more acceptable euphemism for "poor," often used by white ethnic groups who seem to have a hard time saying the p word), the three census tracts in the neighborhood's Lower End held the nation's highest concentration of white poverty. Seventy-five percent of the households in its three housing projects and the low-rent housing around them were families headed by single women. In my housing project, all white and mostly Irish American, 85 percent of residents collected welfare.

In the larger world, though, my neighborhood wasn't known for these statistics. I grew up during its time of greatest notoriety: the 1970s, when South Boston's violent resistance to court-ordered school desegregation flashed across the nation's TV screens. My neighbors appeared, furiously chanting HELL NO WE WON'T GO and throwing rocks at black children who were bused into the neighborhood. Some Southie residents carried out hideous violence, often instigated by politicians who benefited from the neighborhood's insularity and sense of vulnerability to the "social planning" of the big, bad world out there. And for many years to come, the conversation about school desegregation in Boston would focus solely on race—in particular, Southie's racism. Class, not to mention class manipulation by the more powerful, has rarely been discussed.

During the busing riots, the walls between Southie and the bigger world were fortified. Southie became a trap for so many of its young because it met the interests of both our own bigoted right-wing demagogues within Southie and the equally bigoted upper-middle-class white liberals beyond our borders, whose class interests were never threatened by their support for forced busing among the poor. (Phase One of the plan involved only Boston's poorest white and poorest black neighborhoods: South Boston and Roxbury.) Of course violence broke out. Judge Arthur Garrity, who ordered Phase One, and the police in riot gear, who lined our streets on the first day of school, could not possibly have expected anything else.

The year the judge ordered forced busing, 1974, was also the year that Whitey Bulger, known to law enforcement and to the community as a drug dealer and murderer, sealed an agreement with agents in the FBI that gave him carte blanche to control Irish South Boston in exchange for becoming an informant on, among other things, the Italian Mafia across town (bigger fish to the FBI than a less serious-sounding Irish Mafia). Busing may have been the best thing that ever happened to Whitey Bulger. South Boston's young people—especially those in the Lower End's housing projects who could not afford to escape to the Catholic schools—dropped out. The dropouts became lucrative drug customers as well as recruits seeking income via the gangster underworld, with its organized bank heists, truck hijackings, and black-market distribution of goods and services. Poverty + forced busing + drop-outs + a government-protected drug don + a neighborhood code of silence. It all equaled violence and death. Perhaps the conspiracy was not planned among all the power players involved, but it served their interests, not those of my neighbors or of anyone in Roxbury.

I didn't know this, of course, as a child. I just lived it and grew to understand it. Throughout much of the eighties and nineties, with the ascendancy of organized crime, so many families in my neighborhood lost children to violence and the drug trade. As a witness to such atrocities, I'd felt stifled, trapped between a poor white conservative neighborhood's denial and the progressive world's blanket characterization of my neighborhood as the last bastion of white supremacy and bigotry that must be broken. There was no regard for the levels of poverty and violent death in the town, no acknowledgment that we were already broken. I always felt my family's and neighbors' experiences had never been represented or acknowledged. Eventually, I realized that, for my own sake, I needed to take that first step of acknowledging what had happened to us in Southie. But first I had to find the voice to do so. In fact, I had not only to find a voice in a literary sense. I had to learn to speak.

Whenever I am asked that familiar writers' question—"How did you find your voice?"—I have to answer that I've never viewed the process as one that only has to do with writing. It's much bigger. It's about making sense of the world and our experiences in it, as well as making use of those experiences for the sake of others. And for me that began with community-organizing work, long before I ever set out to write a book.

I grew up feeling a stunned speechlessness that trauma specialists have identified as a by-product of violence and terror.* But even more stifling were the mythological narratives determined by powerful players both within and beyond Southie, whether gangsters or politicians, liberals or conservatives. After witnessing so much corruption and death, I tried to suck it up and move on, just like everyone else in the neighborhood. And the more I tried to move on, the more I fell back, suffering from a kind of post-traumatic stress and eventual emotional collapse that manifested psychosomatically. I was convinced that I was sick, that there was something deathly wrong with me, killing me. I was right. But it wasn't physical. It was all of the formative violence I'd witnessed but had been trained not to acknowledge.

* Judith Herman, *Trauma and Recovery: The Aftermath of Violence—from Domestic Abuse to Political Terror* (New York: Basic Books, 1992).

I was fortunate to find my way to the center of activism in Boston, discovering a truth-telling movement of survivors of crime and violence in Boston's African American and Latino neighborhoods. I'd been going to college at the University of Massachusetts, and I kept gravitating to history courses—Irish history, in particular, and the history of colonization in general. Though I didn't realize it at the time, with the study of history I began to discover a *context* for understanding all that I came from, including Southie, a neighborhood that decked itself out in shamrocks and leprechauns often at the expense of understanding its real history, the history of a colonized people who have more in common with their black and brown enemies than they can bear to remember. In the study of history, I also found the context of *class*. Although Americans hardly ever acknowledge class, I could see it in the race riots I'd witnessed at the age of eight, or the constant young deaths in a ghetto neighborhood that would never call itself a ghetto.

While I found this context, though, I still had no place to put it, to make use of it. Then, while taking a criminal justice course (still gravitating, somewhat unconsciously, to the issues of my childhood), I had to do a field study through volunteer work at an agency. Most students in the class picked police, probation, or the district attorney's offices, but I went with a citywide coalition working to reduce violence and crime in Boston by addressing "root causes." Hearing this term used for the first time in relation to violence and crime, I began not only to understand the concept that I was so desperate for, but also to take action. This was the most important stage of empowerment in my life. It gave me my voice.

I started to meet people from the poor, black neighborhoods of Roxbury, Dorchester, and Mattapan, many of whom had lived lives like mine. The only difference was that in black and Latino neighborhoods they were saying the words: *poverty, oppression, corruption, drug trade, murder.* We organized citywide gun buyback programs and gang intervention programs. At rallies, vigils, and press conferences, we told our stories as an instrument of peace. And for the first time in my life, I experienced the liberating power of telling the truth about the violence and deaths in my family.

However, there was one problem with our "citywide" movement. My neighbors were missing from the conversation. I had to take this truth telling home to Southie, though cautiously, since speaking about these things was still not safe. I organized a vigil on All Souls Day 1996, "to remember all those who died too young," as the flyers innocuously stated. I thought no one would come, but the church was flooded with people who had been desperate to come out and simply say the names of their brothers, fathers, sons, daughters who had been murdered, who had overdosed, who had gone missing. And this was the beginning of a truth-telling movement in Southie, the first of many annual All Souls Day vigils.

I witnessed the transformation that takes place when individuals speak truth to power, beginning with just enough voice to utter the name of a family member who had died in a neighborhood that suppressed not only talk of the causes of death but, essentially, acknowledgment of our loved ones' memories, their very existence, and our collective history. I watched survivors go from the simple naming of names at vigils to telling their stories to large groups of people. Witnessing the power of such a movement, both for the personal transformation of the one bearing witness as well as for the greater good of nonviolent activism, I wanted to go even deeper . . . by writing *All Souls*.

Southie had for a long time held some of the city's highest death rates from overdoses, but in the mid- to late 1990s, after Whitey Bulger went on the lam, the neighborhood saw an explosion of heroin overdoses and teen suicides by hanging. It was as if Whitey's absence allowed people to feel again, and for some this meant an even greater need to suppress the pain. Community organizers developed a number of coalitions to deal with the root causes of the crisis. The national media descended on South Boston, this time exposing the poverty rates, drug deaths, and history of crime and silence. People were talking, saying words like "poverty," "corruption," "drug trade," and "murder." As an activist, I was often asked why so many young people were taking their lives. The answer could not be summed up in a sound bite. I knew that these young people had all experienced the life I had: one filled with violence and death, speechless terror, and a further stifling code of silence. And so I knew I had to use the voice I'd acquired in order to encourage others to find their own voices, to tell their own stories, and to make sense of their own histories so that they might move forward.

When I began writing *All Souls* in the late 1990s, the world was witnessing South Africa's Truth and Reconciliation Commission. This was something I knew we'd never have in Boston, whether about race and class issues around busing, or about the deaths from our drug trade, or about our drug lord's immunity from prosecution given by agents of the FBI. Inspired by the commission's title alone, I thought of my writing as engaging in my own personal truth and reconciliation commission, whether or not anyone would ever read it. I just had to tell it.

I first discovered my voice as a student, then used it as an activist and then as a writer. I know that this entire process—finding a context, discovering my voice, and acknowledging what happened—kept me from numbing myself with painkillers (prescribed or otherwise). I know it is why I am not an alcoholic, why I did not kill myself. Writing and activism are, for me, the opposite of suppression, addiction, and self-destruction. But one's voice can be used in as many ways as there are callings in life. Finding one's voice is just as important to a painter, comedian, lawyer, mother, neighbor. In all of these capacities, as with writing, our personal narratives empower us. Our histories and, in particular, our subjective telling of our histories collectively inspire a people's history. What happened—the facts—are not even as important to empowerment and transformation as the telling of what we remember and how we remember it. No history is objective, nor should it pretend to be. In the same way, there are as many stories of busing in Boston, or of life growing up in Southie, as there are in-dividuals who experienced either.

◆ ◆ ◆

When *All Souls* was published, I had lots of support from those who were part of South Boston's burgeoning truth-telling movement, which was growing around the All Souls Day Vigil, and from the coalitions working to address the heroin and suicide epidemics. But much of the neighborhood was still denying the problems. And some—usually career politicians and criminals, both of whom benefited from our closed borders and collective self-deception— had a vested interest in maintaining things just as they always had been. Besides rumors of death threats and the grumblings of politicians, who had looked the other way while the gangsters of this neighborhood profited off our most vulnerable residents, there was a whole new enemy to truth: the real estate brokers and speculators who moved into the vacuum left by gangsters who had begun to either go on the lam or turn state's evidence. A huge profit was to be made on the South Boston waterfront, and talk of gangsters or heroin epidemics was bad for business. So once again, the narratives were reformulated, and the town was presented as "hot" and "trendy," the new SoHo of Boston, ridiculously named "SoBo" by real estate agents.

But there is room for all of the narratives. The only problem is that too many, particularly the poor and voiceless, are left out. At seven in the morning on the day *All Souls* was published, there was a frantic knock on my door. It was a neighbor who ordered me to come downstairs and explain what I'd said about "the rape." I was groggy, trying to remember what rape I might have written about. Then she told me about the time her brother raped a young woman in our stairwell. I had written only about things that I'd witnessed or that affected my life growing up, and I had known nothing about the rape. I told her that if I *had* known, it might very well have been in the book, as I am sure it would have changed me. But the only mention of her family in *All Souls* was in relation to her two younger brothers being saved by my mother. They had been stabbed by their father and were running up the stairwell toward the roof, their father just a flight behind them, when my mother pulled them inside, locked the door on their father, and called 911. One of them collapsed on our floor and was resuscitated by EMTs. This incident, along with all of the chaos of the neighborhood, shaped who I am and of course was in my memoir.

She calmed down and acknowledged painfully that, yes, we "saw a lot of shit growing up in that place." Then she wanted to see a copy of the book for herself, to make sure the rape wasn't in it.

"I don't have a copy," I told her, as I had not yet been sent my complimentary box of books.

"Well, where can I get one?" she asked.

"I guess they're at all the bookstores," I said.

"Well, where's a fucking bookstore?" she yelled at me.

The tragedy of that question brought it all home to me. It seemed unfair: I not only knew where every bookstore in Boston was but knew they were all selling my book. I had found my voice and was using it—but what good was that if others could not? How had I been so fortunate? Why me?

To become an activist, I had to learn that the personal is the political, so I brought my personal experience to bear on the bigger social issues I was advocating. But to become a memoirist, I had to learn that the political is personal, and so I brought it closer to home. I would not have been able to do either without first finding a voice. And that would not have happened—the voice and narrative would not have been shaped—without first discovering context and history. But the empowerment I had found through context and voice was replaced by the guilty knowledge that so many others cannot navigate the narratives and will never have a voice.

A year after the book's publication, I received a call from a Boston juvenile detention facility. One of their teen inmates who was from Old Colony project had persuaded the entire population to read *All Souls* and even organized book discussion groups around it in their AA and NA meetings. They invited me to come speak. I knew when I arrived which kid was from Southie. He was the white one. The black and Latino kids had been shocked to hear that there were white people in projects, on welfare, and experiencing violence as they had. The context of class is as rarely talked about in black and Latino urban communities as anywhere else, yet it is everything. They were relieved to see that the brutality and crime they knew in neighborhoods of color was not something "in the blood." A Latino teenager told me, a white man, "You told my story; you've lived my life."

And some aspects of that life may be slow to change. After my visit, the Southie kid told me that, when he was first incarcerated, the black and Latino kids assumed he was "some rich white kid." "This book saved my life," he said. "They wouldn't even let me speak in here, when they thought I was some white brat." He held up a hardcover copy.

"That's a hardcover," I said. "It's out in paperback now, a lot cheaper. You got it when it was twenty-four bucks?" I said, almost apologizing for the price.

"Nah," he said. "There was a kid going around Southie with a box of them, stolen. Someone got me one for ten bucks, and sent it in."

ELAINE TYLER MAY

Confessions of a Memoir Thief

. . .

WITH AN EXCERPT FROM
Homeward Bound: American Families in the Cold War Era

FROM *Homeward Bound: American Families in the Cold War Era*

Chester Grey was satisfied with his marriage to Nora and rated it high. He claimed that he had sacrificed only "money and financial independence," but gained "a happy home, complete with a loving wife and four children." Nora Grey also reaped what she felt were adequate rewards for her efforts: "A nice home I can run the way I want to. A husband to be a lifetime companion and 'protector.' A fine group of children who keep life from being monotonous. The self-confidence that comes from the knowledge that my husband loves me more than anyone else in the world." For all the world to see, they were a happy 1950s couple. But there was quite a bit the world did not see. At the end of the questionnaire where she could add "anything else" she wished to say, Nora wrote a story of extreme hardship and intense bitterness:

> Much of our trouble has centered around my husband's unwillingness to do work around the house, which he says is my sole responsibility.... This was not too bad until I had the third baby within five years. My husband slept in a different room so as not to be disturbed by her night crying which she did for 5 months. I became so exhausted that I got very little sleep, even when she did, and I had to be up early with the other two little ones.
>
> With the children's care, housework, repairs, leaf raking, snow shoveling, some lawn mowing and making all our clothing (so we could save every penny we could toward a house) I became physically and nervously exhausted. My husband refused to get up with the children or let me stay in bed even one morning.... He said, "You're not human and don't need sleep." ... With the present baby he is extremely different and has slept in her room and cared for her nights whenever I needed rest.

With all this misery, Nora wanted a psychiatrist to help her cope with her situation and make her feel better. But even her desire for professional assistance was out of reach: "I believe I had a nervous breakdown but I knew psychiatric help would be expensive and my husband said, 'Your trouble is all in your head and you don't have to feel this way if you don't want to.' ... For the above reasons we never had another baby until a year ago when I felt I could handle it. Now I feel that at 40 we are too old to take the responsibility of more."

Chester's responses to the questionnaire contained none of the evidence of the domestic strain and distress Nora described, but they revealed that his job was a major source of misery for him. In the question concerning emotional health, he noted, "Extreme depression anxiety and insomnia caused by job. Solved by changing job." Nora, however, was unable to change her job. At the end of her questionnaire, she minimized her suffering and articulated her commitment to her marriage. . . . In a remarkable series of superlative responses, Nora rated her marriage highly successful, "never" considered divorce, would "definitely" marry the same person again, "never" regretted her marriage, and considered it "decidedly more happy than the average."

◆ ◆ ◆

Confessions of a Memoir Thief

I am, by training and occupation, a historian. On the face of it, there is really no reason for me to steal memoirs. History and memoir are both interpretive arts. Both genres use carefully selected fragments of the past—memories, documents, events—to tell a story. In that sense, memoirists and historians mine similar sites and go through similar processes to construct their understandings of the past. Their work is refracted largely through each writer's particular place in the present. Each practitioner, driven by individual passions, questions, and concerns, crafts a portrait of the past that blends historical memory, personal experience, and interpretive analysis. Both write creative nonfiction—although that term is usually applied to memoir and not to history.

But the two genres diverge around viewpoint. Memoir is expressed in the first person, showing a particular life in a particular context. History is told in the third person, generalizing from many particular stories in an attempt to create a larger narrative about change over time. Emotion plays different roles in the writing of

memoir and history. Memoir is generally understood as a highly personal rendering of the past, refracted through private experience,
feelings, and relationships. History is usually grounded in public life,
considered somehow objective and detached from emotion. But is
memoir really entirely private and subjective and history completely
public and detached? People live public and private lives, often intertwined. The distinction between the two realms is often overstated
or artificial. Memoirists and historians till the same soil. So why would
a historian steal the personal stories of others? It does not seem necessary. Not every historian does.

But I do.

I will try to explain what drove me to such a questionable activity
by writing a brief memoir of myself as a historian—a task that is quite
foreign to those of us trained in the methods and language of historical scholarship. First of all there is that troubling pronoun "I."
Most historians learn to bury the first person pronoun. I (yes, I) do
not allow my students to use it. "Assert your argument," I tell them,
"history is not about your opinion." It is not as though there is no
author, or some vague royal "we" (I don't allow that one, either). It
is rather the presumed voice of authority, the distanced and objective
expert whose words and interpretations need not be owned other
than on the title page. The invisible "I" is something of a fiction—
or rather a convention of writing historical scholarship. Of course,
what historians do with the bits and pieces of the past they select and
arrange is uniquely their own. If their work was not based on original ideas and analyses, it would not be considered scholarship. Their
writings would simply be narratives of the past, which is not the
same as history, just as a narrative of a life is not a memoir.

It began simply enough. I dove into history in the 1960s and 1970s,
when historians were turning away from the study of leaders and
other elites, of wars and battles, and discovering ordinary people as
agents of history. This new social history, as we called it, reflected
the turmoil in society as well as in my soul. Those who had been
buried in earlier renditions of history suddenly surfaced. Women's

history, African American history, labor and immigration history, gay and lesbian history, Chicano and American Indian history, Asian American history—all began to develop as legitimate fields of historical inquiry. At the same time, areas of life and institutions that had previously been considered timeless, eternal, or outside of history opened up to historical investigation. Family, sexuality, gender, race—aspects of life once seen as unchanging or rooted in biological processes—came to be understood as historically constructed. The institution of the family had a history. Sex had a history. Historians began to discover new ways of understanding the past in which the distinction between the public and the private became blurred or even evaporated. Historians began to discover emotion.

The study of history came to embrace the lives and feelings of those previously ignored by historians: ordinary people, not those who have already made their mark. We would write "history from the bottom up." The civil rights movement quickly generated a rich historical literature on African Americans. The feminist movement sparked an explosion in women's history. It was an exciting, heady time to be entering the field.

There were, however, some major challenges, mostly having to do with sources. In truth, historians have often drawn on memoirs in their work. There is nothing new or nefarious about that. People write memoirs for the public record. Or they deposit their personal papers in archives, in order for those documents to be viewed and used—by historians or whoever might be interested. These are memoirs freely given. They do not need to be stolen. The problem is that the people who thus give their memoirs are usually members of the elite. These types of memoirs and papers generally do not help social historians write history from the bottom up, since these folks tend to be at the top, not the bottom. Finding memoirs of people who have not given them to the public requires some stealth.

I first learned the art of sleuthing for memoirs when I was in graduate school at UCLA. In a seminar taught by one of the social history pioneers, we were assigned to write a paper based on records of ordinary people. Our challenge was to bypass published works and the manuscript collections and libraries where papers of notable people were housed. Los Angeles was our archive. Each of us went out exploring the various nooks and crannies where records of ordinary people were collected.

I hit the streets. I took the freeway to downtown Los Angeles, struggled to find a cheap place to park, hiked several blocks to the Los Angeles County Archives. I spent a long and weary day looking at public records. Birth records contained quite a bit of information: mothers' and fathers' names, occupations, places of birth, nationality, race, age, and so forth. Death records also contained useful information about ordinary individuals. There were also documents that recorded property acquisition, business records, and all sorts of transactions. But these records had no stories, no real people, no emotion. Just numbers and bits of data. I imagined myself making charts with categories and checking off little boxes for hours on end. I would die of boredom before I could write one word of history—and what could I write without stories?

Then I discovered court records. To be precise, I discovered divorce records. There I found real stories, full of flesh and blood, full of drama. Feminism had drawn me to history. I knew that the personal was political. The issues that sparked my passion for history were grounded in feminist issues: women's experiences and changing roles, the personal world of marriage and family, changing sexual norms and behaviors, changing leisure activities and consumer culture, the impact of the women's rights movement—all of those issues were at the center of the struggles of dissolving marriages, and there they were in the public record. I had found my gold mine: a treasure trove of brief but exquisitely distilled memoirs.·

Divorce court records, of course, are not memoirs in the strict sense of the word. They are mediated by lawyers and written for a particular purpose, different from that of the memoirist. But testimonies in divorce court have quite a bit in common with memoir. They are drawn from personal memory and filled with emotion. They are constructed from selected bits of past experience, connected to particular events in the couple's married life, and put together to make a point: my spouse is guilty. In the years before no-fault divorce, there had to be a guilty party. Fortunately for me, California considered marital crimes such as "mental cruelty" as grounds for divorce. The records were thus often very detailed and open-ended. Stories of betrayal, disappointment, and anguish may well have been written for the public record, but they were not meant for the historian's probing eyes. Parties to divorce cases hoped for a decision in their favor, and they expected that their depositions would be safely hidden away on some obscure shelf and never looked at again.

My research was focused on the Progressive Era, the years between 1880 and 1920, when the women's rights movement gained momentum and women finally achieved the right to vote, when the "new woman" appeared on the urban scene to challenge the middle-class mores of the past, when sexual behavior was changing so rapidly that activities previously considered scandalous had become the norm. All of those issues came to life in these accounts of the trials and tribulations of divorcing couples, and the line between the private and the public crumbled. One minute I felt like a kid with my fingers in a cookie jar; the next minute I fancied myself a spy whose magnifying glass had just come across the hidden clue that would solve the mystery I was filled with sheepish delight. Take the travails of the Linganfields, for example:

> In the Superior Court of Los Angeles in 1920, Lorimer Linganfield, a respectable barber, filed for divorce. Although his wife, Marsha, held him in "high regard and esteem as her husband," there were "evidences of indiscretion" in her conduct. She wore a new bathing suit, "designed especially for the purpose of exhibiting to the public the shape and form of her body." To his further humiliation, she was "beset with a desire to sing and dance at cafes and restaurants for the entertainment of the public." When Lorimer complained about her "appetite for beer and whisky" and extravagant tastes for luxury, she replied that he was "not the only pebble on the beach, she had a

millionaire 'guy' who would buy her all the clothes, automobiles, diamonds and booze that she wanted." The ultimate insult was her refusal to have sexual intercourse, claiming that she did not want any "dirty little brats around her." The judge was sympathetic. Lorimer Linganfield won his suit—and Marsha won her freedom.*

Here was everything I wanted to uncover: changing gender roles, public and private morals, sexual behavior, reproductive patterns, and expectations for marriage. Poor Lorimer divorced Marsha for the same reasons he married her: she was a sexy flapper full of fun and excitement. To a fault, it turned out.

So I became a memoir thief and a historian at the same time. Although it seemed slightly underhanded to take the personal miseries of people of my grandparents' generation and use them for the lofty goals of writing feminist history, I felt justified because I was writing history from the bottom up. The best I could do to assuage my guilt (was I now the guilty party?) was to treat these documents with sensitivity and respect—to use the substance without abusing it. I did not need to expose people's real names, even though these were public records and doing so would break no law. To protect my subjects' privacy, I used pseudonyms (and case record numbers for the purpose of citation), a practice I have held to ever since. I also needed to take these individuals on their own terms. This is an important aspect of writing history. Although we all write from the present, we must avoid the temptation to read the past through the present. Memoir writers face the same challenge. Memories, like historical documents, need to be situated and interpreted in their proper moment. We cannot escape the hindsight that comes with writing about the past—in fact, hindsight is essential. But we need to do our best to move our imaginations into the time frame of our subjects.

My sleuthing gave me what I needed for both the dissertation and

* Divorce Case D492, Los Angeles County Archives, 1920, in May, *Great Expectations: Marriage and Divorce in Post-Victorian America* (Chicago: University of Chicago Press, 1980), 1.

the degree. As often happens with such adventures, it became somewhat habit forming. The Los Angeles divorce cases satisfied my curiosity about my hometown, but could I make a claim for a larger national story? After all, as skeptical questioners at job interviews insisted, Los Angeles is its own thing. Especially when it comes to matters of sex, love, marriage, consumer culture, and the like. Under the hot lights of interrogation at a job interview at Princeton University, when asked how I could claim much of anything on the basis of records of a bunch of deviant turn-of-the-century California misfits, I blurted out my confession: you are right. I promised that before my work landed between two hard covers, I would do some research in a more "normal" place. Reassured, they hired me, and I explored the divorce records of New Jersey. The stories were not so different, even on the farm:

> Maude and Andrew Grossman married in 1917 and lived on Andrew's parents' farm until 1920 when Maude walked out. According to the state interviewer, Maude was "tired of living on the farm." Andrew explained, "My wife frequently complained that she was dissatisfied to live [on] our farm. She was fond of moving pictures and wanted to go [to her hometown] most of her time, where things were more active." Andrew's father supported his son: "Andrew has lived on our farm since his wife deserted him. Andrew is a boy of good habits. He never uses liquor or tobacco. He is a church member and a good boy. He has always been industrious and works every day. He has always been a good worker. My farm is plentifully stocked and it could not be possible for anyone to live on my farm and not have plenty to eat."

Plenty to eat was not enough to satisfy Maude's cravings, so she took off for the bright lights of the city. This case and others demonstrated how changes in women's roles, sexual mores, consumer tastes, job opportunities, and urban life ratcheted up the expectations for marriage, leading to higher levels of disappointment when those expectations were not met.

Having gathered a bundle of memoir vignettes from New Jersey as well as Los Angeles, I wrote them up and sent them to my editor at the University of Chicago Press, who figured that if you averaged the East Coast and the West Coast you got the heartland and published my book.

But that was not the end of it. My habit was formed, and divorce records were no longer enough. I moved on to a bigger story, from my grandparents' generation to that of my parents, and I did something even more brazen: I stole from another memoir thief.

It was one thing to figure out why the American divorce rate went from almost nothing in 1880 to the highest in the world by 1920. It was quite another to untangle the story of the baby boom after World War II. I found lots of great material in the usual public records and evidence from popular culture and the prescriptive literature. But I couldn't find any real people behind the glittery celebration of family life in Cold War America. No emotion. So I began sleuthing again and found another unexpected cache of booty. Tucked away in the Henry Murray Center at Radcliffe College, next to the famed Schlesinger Library women's history archives, was a glorious collection, the equivalent of a historian's vintage store: gently used data from an earlier era. A social psychologist had made a longitudinal study of middle-class married couples who filled out lengthy, open-ended questionnaires from the late 1930s to the mid-1950s, revealing the intimate details of their lives. After publishing a few brief articles on psychological development in marriage, the initial collector had dropped his lovely material into the recycle bin. Score!

Some pieces of the data set were perfect, including questions on gender roles, household tasks, work experiences, consumer patterns, preferences for numbers of children and how those preferences changed over time, and consumer spending patterns. But the original investigator, true to his era, was not interested in the same questions that interested me. I was baffled that a detailed survey that included dozens of questions on sexual behavior did not ask one question about politics, not even what political party the informants joined, or even if they voted. Welcome to the 1950s. Nevertheless, the surveys revealed in richly textured detail how these couples interacted, lived, loved, and built their families in the years of the baby boom. They were not meant for my eyes. They were not even meant for each other's eyes. Husbands and wives filled out the questionnaires alone and sent them to the investigator. Putting these surveys side by side, it was clear that some of these folks, although married to each other, were in different marriages.

In any case, I had my set of memoirs, history from the bottom up, filled with my substance of choice: emotion. If any group of Americans had access to the American dream after World War II, it was these affluent, white New England suburbanites. They taught me how much distance there was between the dream and the reality. Take the case of Maria and Norman Kimball, who married after breaking the rules of midcentury sexual propriety:

> "I have concluded that my husband has deep emotional conventionality such that the attitudes our 'free love' experience fostered undermined his respect and admiration for me. . . . I have been faithful, but doubt if he believes this." Nevertheless, Maria claimed that her marriage gave her "the purely female pleasure of having a husband whose behavior is never an embarrassment, who never lets one down in public, never vents malicious humor, and whose ideas and attitudes rarely jar one's own beliefs. In outside contacts, we work like a well-oiled team. It may be wryly amusing at times, but there's some satisfaction in having acquaintances envy one's apparent compatibility." Using explicit cold-war terminology, she continued, "Each retreats from any sphere of influence in which the other develops an interest. . . . I don't suppose either of us is too satisfied with this noncooperative impasse, but it works. In fact, it works very well. So long as we maintain a state of breakdown in communication, we get along fine. Crazy, isn't it? Yet these last few years I've come to believe that however irrational a human relationship may be, if it works, it's valid."[*]

---

* Case 244, Kelly Longitudinal Study, in May, *Homeward Bound: American Families in the Cold War Era* (New York: Basic Books, 1988), 101, 182–85.

The Kimballs' marriage worked until the 1970s, when the feminist movement and changing attitudes toward divorce made it possible for them to give up the charade.

I swiped the Kimballs' story, and hundreds more like it, and published my second book. I then turned to our nation's obsession with reproduction (particularly Americans' preoccupation with the procreative proclivities of other people). I began a book about reproductive outsiders: the childless. But much as I searched, I could not find any records anywhere that gave me insight into the experiences and feelings of the childless. Many pundits, professionals, and activists wrote about childlessness: infertility specialists, social workers, eugenicists, "childfree" advocates, environmentalists. But I was unable to find the stories of ordinary people who were childless by choice, chance, or even coercion. No stories, no emotion. Finally, hooked as I was, I had no choice but to persuade people to write memoirs for me. I didn't really go about this under false pretenses; I used the typical author query placed in newspapers around the country. Tell me your stories of childlessness, I begged; I am writing a book, and I need the stories of real people. I promised I would not use real names. People responded. They got nothing in return except the satisfaction of expressing their feelings and experiences. Hundreds of rich, wonderful letters arrived in my mailbox. Nearly everyone who wrote to me assumed I was childless. The infertile expressed sadness for my pain. The "childfree" congratulated me on my good sense to be among them, the ones who resisted social pressure and lived happy, unencumbered lives. None suspected that I had three children. No matter— they volunteered what I needed for my story: the emotional as well as physical costs of being outside the normative pronatalist culture. Patricia Painter, for example, wrote of her struggle with infertility:

> For a while I tried telling people, "Oh, we're trying." Oh God, people were chuckling or laughing and saying, "Oh, isn't that all the fun." Yeah, it's loads of fun going to the doctor all the time and spending tremendous amounts of money, and having all these painful tests, horrible things, and not being able to have sex normally, loads of

fun, let me tell you how much fun I'm having. Anyway, it was terrible. Those comments were terrible.*

People like her poured out their hearts and their stories. Voilà, a third book.

I have built a career on the memoirs of others—unsuspecting people who deposited their personal stories in places where I could steal them with ease. But there is a little secret here that may be obvious by now. Through the stories of unwitting memoirists, I have investigated the worlds of my own family past. Is it a matter of mere coincidence that I found myself passionately interested in the rapidly changing urban life that my Jewish immigrant grandparents encountered when they arrived in New York City in the early twentieth century? Is it any surprise that I next became fascinated with the middle-class suburban world my parents entered when they contributed my three siblings and me to the baby boom? And surely it is relevant that as the daughter of a birth-control-activist mother and an infertility-specialist father I became interested in the culture of reproduction.

Perhaps my little secret is the secret of most historians. We disavow the first person in our writing and bury the "I" in our data and interpretations. Yet like those who write memoir, we are interested in the past viewed through our own eyes. In my case, I have managed to investigate the environments of my family over three generations. So have I stolen all these minimemoirs in order to write my own megamemoir? I am a historian. I am a memoir thief. And finally, I turn out to be . . . a memoirist.

---

* Quoted in May, *Barren in the Promised Land: Childless Americans and the Pursuit of Happiness* (New York: Basic Books, 1995), 13.

ALICE KAPLAN

Lady of the Lake

. . .

WITH AN EXCERPT FROM
French Lessons: A Memoir

FROM *French Lessons: A Memoir*

Teaching, I discover, is not really about my French, my body, and whether or not they're correct. It's about generating words—other people's words. Making people change, making them make mistakes, making them care and not care, making them sensitive, but not oversensitive, to the nuances of language. Making them take risks. It is physical, shockingly physical. Not just because I am there, walking across the room so their eyes won't fall asleep, but because I, Madame, have to make their mouths work. I walk up to a student and I take her mouth in my hand; I arrange it in the shape of a perfect O. Too close, a little too close to repeat.

Occasionally I divide our bodies in half, our left side speaking English, our right side speaking French so we can feel the difference in our posture, our hands, our muscles. Our English side slouches, while our French side is crisp and pointed. In English we gesture downwards with one hand, in French our entire arm is in a constant upward movement. With our French side, we shake imaginary dirt from our hand with a repeated flick of the wrist, to show we are impressed, scandalized, amused. This is interesting, to be double like this with them, and funny enough for comfort. Also from Capretz I learn to teach tricks that no one ever taught me for making French sounds. For the "r," gargling with mouthwash to feel the vibration in your throat. This tells you where the French "r" is, until finally you can do it without the aid. Making the "u" sound—the "u" in "tu" or "fondue" or "bu," that most French of French sounds—is a three-part pedagogy. First you say "o" with your mouth in a perfect round (as though you were going to peck someone on the cheek), then "eee" (with your mouth stretched out in a horizontal smile like a trout, or a wide pumpkin), then a combination of the two: with your mouth in the shape of a perfect "o," you say "eee." The sound "u" comes out. This works well.

The Capretz method depends on students not making things up, it teaches them to absorb and recycle ready-made bits of language. It asks them to listen to the tapes in the lab and let the story of the week sink in, like a hit song that you listen to in the car on your way into work and end up knowing in spite of yourself. This is hard. American students want A's for originality. They can't believe that language isn't theirs to remake. They compensate with theatricality: by the end of a good semester a Capretz class is a repertory theater, the students, method actors. The extroverts learn French so well by this method that it frightens me.

This is what teaching is like, too, knowing that you are teaching better than you yourself ever learned, that you can get more from your students than you were ever capable of giving. Teaching, if it succeeds, is dealing with the fact that some of those hams will be better than you are.

◆ ◆ ◆

Lady of the Lake

An autobiography, says the critic Philippe Lejeune in a now classic essay on the subject, is a retrospective account of a person's life, written in the first person, in which that person tries to make sense of his or her life. The autobiographer makes a pact with the reader, usually stated explicitly in the first pages of the book, to tell the truth. Whether it's really possible to tell the truth about oneself is a separate issue. What counts in an auto-biography, according to Lejeune's theory, is a commitment to honesty.*

As the author of a memoir called French Lessons, *published fifteen years ago, I can say in hindsight that this commitment to telling the truth about oneself is both the most exciting and the most elusive aspect of auto-biographical writing. Writing about yourself is a high-wire balancing act between revelation and a need to set bounds, to respect your own need for privacy and the right to privacy of others. If you achieve what the genre of autobiography asks of you, you may be giving away too much. That's the trouble with memoir. If I had realized this when I wrote* French Les-sons— *if, for example, I could have anticipated how disturbing it would be to meet total strangers who felt that they knew me—I might never have written it. I'm glad I did, glad I didn't anticipate the sense of alienation that memoir publishing (as opposed to memoir writing) brings with it. For my memoir project, I wanted to take on two genres, memoir and history,*

---

* Philippe Lejeune, "The Autobiographical Pact," in *On Autobiography,* trans. Katherine Leary (Minneapolis: University of Minnesota Press, 1989), 3–30.

and put them in a dynamic relationship with one another. Since I'm a historian of memoir (as well as a memoirist), I find it compelling to think about exactly what a memoir writer won't or can't say.

Some unfinished business of my own set me on the journey to write specifically about Brenda Ueland, a memoirist close to home. In French Lessons I had written about one aspect of myself: the self who wanted to escape into another language, who wanted to leave home. And a self who, in the course of studying the history of France, was drawn to national secrets.

A memoir can never achieve a total truthfulness, in part because you the author have to decide which part of yourself to narrate. Selves, as Brenda Ueland understood, are multiform creatures. In my imagination there has always been another, unwritten self—not the person who lives in France but the one always drawn back home, to Minnesota. And there, in the mental world of that self, resides Brenda Ueland, the Minnesota icon, a kind of mental placeholder for another, potential memoir, which might have been my "Minnesota Lessons." And this Brenda Ueland happened to be a memoir writer of renown, as well as a person who liked to think about what it means to write and what it means to tell the truth.

My memories of Ueland led me to do the same kind of work I have always done on French topics: to go to the archives, to study the way she worked, and to look at what she decided to leave in and leave out of her own "tell all" writing. To play the historian to her confessional prose. History and memoir, much like biography and autobiography, are sibling rivals: each wants the upper hand in storytelling. Brenda Ueland liked to say that doing research was just a way of avoiding one's true feelings. What a perfect foil for the academic writer that I am! Oversized emotion, bragging, and extreme subjectivity can also be avoidance tactics—they were often hers. In writing about her, I hoped to figure something out about each of us.

Brenda Ueland is someone I can conjure easily: an ancient woman with a gnarled face and white hair walking very fast around Lake Harriet. I must have seen her making her way around that Minneapolis lake a thousand times, hunched over, a funny cap pulled down over her forehead. Today people still go on about her—the eccentric feminist who played tennis in the nude, the legendary writer, the old Norwegian troll who climbed Pike's Peak in her eighties. Connie, my friend who grew up on the other side of Lake Harriet, visited the writer at the end of her life and got me to read her books. From reading them and talking about her, I've made Brenda Ueland part of the landscape I visit in my imagination every day, the landscape of my childhood.

We were children in the 1960s. In those days, the park board hadn't gentrified the area around Lake Harriet, and the plant life grew at will. The walking paths were muddy and unkempt. Wild branches from the skinny trees growing along the shoreline stuck straight out over the water. Connie and I used them as our balance beams. We knew that if we fell, the water would only come up to our ankles or knees—water so clear you could see the minnows and the sand at the bottom. No pollution, no milfoil weeds then.

The three lakes in the southern part of Minneapolis are so close they almost touch. When I was a student, I could walk from home to school in a little over an hour if I followed the boulevards around them. That was my universe. Lake Harriet was my home lake, the lake I liked to swim across. After Harriet came Lake Calhoun, a flat mirror, except on windy days when the waves looked like impressionist brush strokes. This may be why, when I was a child, I thought all impressionist reproductions were scenes of Minneapolis. Finally came Lake of the Isles, the only man-made lake, too muddy and weedy for swimming but civilized and austere, with two islands in it and mansions on the manicured grass slopes that surround it on every side. If you lived in that world and even thought about being a writer, the first thing you wanted to write about was the beauty of those lakes.

Brenda Ueland was born on Lake Calhoun in 1891 and spent the last years of her life in a house perched just beyond Lake Harriet, in the neighborhood called Linden Hills. She was the fourth child in a family of four brothers and three sisters. Her father, a Norwegian immigrant who had begun his working life as a day laborer, attended night law school and rose to prominence as a judge and legal counsel. Her mother, an important public figure in her own right, was the founder of the Minnesota League of Women Voters. Although conversations in her home were lively and progressive, and the atmosphere warm, young Brenda suffered from her busy mother's absence.

She could see the lake from her bedroom, and throughout her long and varied career as a writer, the sentences she wrote about the landscape of Minneapolis are among her most beautiful. She had a lyrical gift that reminds me of Fitzgerald—her effortlessly lovely sentences give the impression that she wrote as she breathed. The lakes were the medium for all her senses, especially hearing:

> And sometimes at night we did hear unutterably sad cries, sad lost cries for help: screech owls. And in spring there were loons calling. And on the other side of Lake Calhoun, a mile and a half away, there were train tracks. On summer nights when the lake was still or there was a slight breeze from the north, we could hear for a long time that incredibly beautiful, soft roar of a train, coming from far away.

Trains for people in the middle west, she explained, were like ships for people on the coast—they meant "travel, escape, leaving home, sadness, freedom, adventure. . . . They come from the wild plains of Dakota and Montana, and they go on and on and across the world, and you get on one and perhaps you never come back."

Brenda went by train to college in New York and returned home in 1913 to start work in the newspaper business. In 1915, she left by train for New York again and stayed there for fifteen years. She worked for magazines, lived a bohemian existence in Greenwich Village, took lovers, married and divorced, gave birth to a daughter, Gabrielle, and made a modest living as a freelance writer. After her mother died in 1930, she came home to Minneapolis to her father's house. At the end of his life, when the weather was good, they walked together:

We walked slowly way around the lake. I think it was spring, for I seem to smell that day and remember that we stepped around soft muddy places occasionally, as though there was still some frost being thawed from the ground. We went to the outlet on the far side, and beyond that to the path that leaves the road and follows the lake along a thicket. Then back.

Walking around the lakes was her ideal setting not only for conversation, but for contemplation. She was convinced that, unless she walked long hours every day, her thinking became something petty and dull. Her brain needed good outdoor air. This was a hard principal to stick to in Minnesota, but winter didn't stop her, or so she bragged in a diary entry from 1936, when she was already forty-four:

This noon I went around Lake Harriet and two miles farther. It is more than 18 below zero. But I am warm. I wear as always my burglar suit, and under it two layers of wool underwear, and two layers of truck driver's mittens under horsehide, a Norwegian cap with a visor. I am warm in this cold, though the air is a sword in the lungs. It is very beautiful. The sun is a blare of gold in the pure blue sky and everything is so still, golden, pallidly golden. No one is out except an occasional snow plow or milk truck. The drivers stare at me, smiling through their closed-in glass cabs. Two dogs come out barking at me, but overjoyed to have a human being out and walking, and they frolic around me, their joy overcoming their hostility and their barking indignation.

Even when she was a very old woman, there is something young about her writing, as though she's still a teenager, figuring herself out. The passage above, along with other diary entries, formed the backbone of her 1938 memoir, which she called *Me*, a pioneering book, one of the first in an autobiographical tradition, now so central to American writing, that gives value to everyday experience. Ueland wants to account for her relationships, to describe her working life, her endless quest for discipline and for understanding the world. *Me* shows her lyrical gifts, her penchant for bragging, her self-absorption, and, in the end, a knowledge of her own shortcomings that endears her to the reader.

Brenda Ueland's complaints about the business of writing surface in the part of *Me* devoted to the late 1930s. This was still the golden age of the short story, when magazines like *Collier's* and the *Saturday Evening Post*, each with over a million subscribers, published new stories every week. In the thick of the Depression, without enough money for books, people bought magazines. Stars like F. Scott Fitzgerald could make $3,600 from the sale of a single story, and $1,500 wasn't an unusual fee for a lesser-known writer—the equivalent of $12,000 today. You could make enough from selling stories to support yourself over the long haul of working on a novel.

Ueland had had a good run of success in this thriving magazine world: a stint as an editor at *Liberty* magazine in New York, a dozen or more articles published in *Harper's, Ladies' Home Journal, Saturday Evening Post*. Then suddenly, it seemed, the stories she wanted to write weren't marketable. She began to teach a class in writing at a branch of the Minneapolis YWCA. And she began writing about her experience in the class, in light of her own disappointing rejections. Most of her students had no writing experience, and the less they had written, or so it seemed to her, the better, the fresher their stories seemed to be. This was a revelation. She described one student, Mrs. B, who had done a great deal of writing and revising, and whose prose was dull and mechanical. "Stock prose," Ueland called it, and from Mrs. B's story, she derived a maxim: "The more you wish to describe a Universal the more minutely and truthfully you must describe a Particular." Don't try to make it sound smooth, she advised. Write "with exquisite and completely detached exactness and truthfulness. Look at the person and just say what you see, even if it sounds like a catalogue."

Ueland might have been talking about herself. She had made a name, and a living, writing personal essays about women. Her articles had titles like "Fat or Thin Women" and "Dressmakers, Clients and Husbands." Her nonfiction opinion pieces already had hints of the uncompromising quality that would become her trademark, but she wasn't having fun with them. She complained in *Me* of driven perfectionism, of polishing her magazine submissions fifty times. Much of her fiction was conventional, with artificial society settings, girls fighting with their parents or falling in and out of love. There's also an anorexic tone to much of her magazine writing on diet and weight, a disgust for the female body and a drive for self-abnegation that would surface through her life, aftereffects of an overweight childhood.

But there are also a few wonderful stories, such as her 1927 "I Mean Marriage Is Terrible!" published in the *Delineator,* where a bohemian expatriate with literary pretensions pities her college friend who has decided to marry and settle down. The expatriate wastes her time posing as an avant-garde writer in Paris, only to return home to discover that her boring married friend has written two powerful novels and sold one of them to the movies. The story, narrated in the first person, may be a thinly veiled send-up of Brenda's rivalry with her older sister, Anne, a writer who settled into a conventional bourgeois life with her doctor husband in Connecticut. It's a hilarious spoof on artistic pretensions that brings out Brenda's impatience with frauds and her ability to mock herself.

Among Ueland's nonfiction from the 1930s, one essay stands out for similar reasons. "Grass Widows: As Told to Brenda Ueland"* takes the point of view and voice of a man describing the devastating effect of alimony payments on his life. By this time Ueland herself had divorced, and you can sense an extraordinary generosity and sympathy in her ability to write from a point of view so opposite her own.

Her writing class at the YWCA made her look back at all her literary efforts in the 1920s and 1930s in a new light. From this retrospection she produced her first book, *If You Want to Write.* Its credo was straightforward, populist. "All writing is alive and interesting if

* *Saturday Evening Post,* January 30, 1932.

it comes out freely and truly. What makes it dead and tiresome is the so-called 'literary effort,' a kind of striving to be effective, instead of just opening your mouth and telling what you have to say."

Her advice was simple: don't listen to the critics, don't listen to the teachers, don't try to be literary. At age forty-seven, this was Ueland's manifesto and proof that she had finally come to terms with what she needed to do to be true to herself as a writer.

When *If You Want to Write* was first published in 1938 by Putnam's, the few reviews were skeptical. The *Saturday Review of Literature* attacked the idea that most people can write, complaining that Ueland was "holding out false hopes to the untalented."* Let the mediocre writers stick to reading, they advised. But when Graywolf Press reissued her book in 1987, in an era when more and more Americans were taking writing classes and when self-help books of all kinds had become a niche in the literary marketplace, it became an instant best seller. No one remembers Brenda Ueland's stories or memoir, but the new edition of *If You Want to Write* has sold more than 300,000 copies, and it's still selling steadily.

If You Want to Write is a beguiling book, bristling with the energy of Ueland's voice, which has given thousands of people with no elite education or literary culture permission and encouragement to express themselves—and specific strategies for getting down to work. And for professional writers, it's a healthy corrective to self-conscious prose and perfectionism. At its foundation is a contradiction: don't listen to teachers, the author warns, and proceeds to teach. This supremely didactic book is full of Brenda Ueland's common sense, as well as elegant wisdom from William Blake and Alfred de Musset.

But there is also something missing in *If You Want to Write.* For all its energy and gumption, it is willfully naïve about literature and the literary enterprise. Ueland is so enthusiastic about feelings and originality in writing that she ignores, or denies, the part of writing that

* *Saturday Review of Literature,* July 30, 1938.

is based on imitation, that derives its strength from literary tradition—the part of writing that involves copying models from the past, or imitating what you admire. Despite her admiration for past writers, anything having to do with writing in a specific genre, according to age-old rules, is suspect. Her version of literary creation is especially shallow when it comes to her chapter on Renaissance noblemen, who wrote sonnets, according to Ueland, strictly to express their true feelings for their lady friends. There's no room in her manifesto for the artfulness of imitation that was essential to Renaissance poetry.

If You Want to Write sets up a dichotomy: On the side of good writing is originality, honesty, spontaneity, and true feelings. On the side of bad writing is the marketplace, conformism, and stock prose. But the reality of writing is much more complicated since, good or bad, it can come from the heart or from the most guileful imitations of age-old conventions. And this takes us right to the year 1949 and a chapter of her life that Ueland never included in the thousands of pages she wrote.

A decade after publishing *If You Want to Write*, Ueland copied, word for word, four or five paragraphs from an essay about a cowboy published in *Life* magazine and inserted them into a short story about a cowboy she sold to *Collier's* magazine. Her copying was discovered and she was exposed. I had heard the story whispered, in literary conversations among friends in Minnesota—whispered in parlors, as people used to say. When pressed, no one could tell me exactly where or what she had plagiarized, or even when it happened, only that her transgression had been revealed in the *New Yorker*. As far as anyone knew, she had never written about the incident.

I was fascinated by the idea that a writer so committed to originality, a person whose legend is so bound up with spontaneous creativity, had herself once been accused of copying. Here was one of those contradictions in a writer's life that could go to the very heart of the literary enterprise. I had a hundred questions about what had happened. I remembered the passage in *Me* where she confesses her penchant for lying: "A life-long struggle," she wrote. "An ethical struggle that is not over yet by any means." You could read the 1938 memoir as a promise that there might be trouble ahead.

I decided to investigate. *Decided* is not really the right word: I was driven. I was filled with the kind of energy that makes me feel like a student again, allows me to spend hours at a time in the library stacks, gives me a sense of urgency that seems to dilate time.

I started with chronology, with the assumption that if Ueland plagiarized, there must be a reason and that the reason must have had something to do with her own history as a writer, with what had happened to her after the enormous productivity of the late 1930s. Between her banner years, 1938 and 1939, which saw the publication of *If You Want to Write* and *Me*, and 1949, the year of her plagiarism, Brenda Ueland published only two national magazine articles, a 1941 essay for *Collier's* on the Royal Norwegian Air Force ("Fighting Wings for Norway") and an ode to listening for *Ladies' Home Journal* called "Tell Me More," based on a call-in radio show that Ueland did in Minneapolis. Magazines were in trouble in the 1940s; circulations were plummeting. *Collier's*, which bought Ueland's tainted short story in 1949, was on a downward slide, and it would fold six years later.

Ueland was fifty-eight years old in 1949. She had married and divorced, raised a daughter, married again, taught a generation of aspiring young writers in Minneapolis, published two books, and imposed her cheerful eccentricity on her neighbors. Her walking path around Lake Harriet was well trodden by now, the daily walks as long as nine miles, winter and summer. She liked to say she went around the lake twice—once for her body, once for her soul. Her father had been dead for fifteen years. Her daughter Gaby, now twenty-eight, had married and left home.

Ueland's second husband, Manus McFadden, was the editor of the *Minneapolis Times,* which had published Brenda's regular column, "What Goes on Here," since 1941. Every column featured a sketch of

Brenda in profile, boyish and hawk nosed with her thick helmet of hair. Then in 1948, the *Times* went out of business—absorbed by the more powerful *Minneapolis Tribune*. Seven years of steady newspaper work, then nothing. During the period when she was writing the story that got her in trouble, Brenda Ueland was at loose ends. In her 1948 diary, she vowed to write eight stories in eight weeks.

In 1949, after a dry spell of seven years with national magazines, Ueland finally sold the short story "Men's Tears" to *Collier's* for $1,500, which must have seemed like a small fortune to Brenda and her husband, who were strapped for cash. "Men's Tears" was an oddity— it was, by her own standards, exactly what she advised against: stock prose, the bad old habit she had denounced ten years earlier in *If You Want To Write*.

She couldn't have chosen a magazine whose requirements for stories were more formulaic. *Collier's* published at least one romance a week, with either a detective or a society or a western theme. Her version was faithful to the norm: In Dry Root County, Montana, Larry Brown and Bashful Jack Connell, who competed in the rodeo, vied for the same yellow-haired girl, Dolores Olson. Larry Brown was all bravura, but Bashful Jack finally won the girl in the end because he cried when he told her he loved her. Even the one offbeat touch in "Men's Tears," the vision of a weeping cowboy, was as old as Odysseus's return to Ithaca.

"Men's Tears" might have been just a weak moment in an otherwise spirited career, if she hadn't copied from a source as visible as *Life*.

With the Internet, almost any project can develop in a matter of hours. One person central to the plagiarism story came right into view on my laptop screen: Claude Stanush, author of the 1946 *Life* magazine profile that Brenda Ueland pilfered, is featured today on a website he shares with his daughter Michele, also a writer. I called her, and she arranged for me to call him at his home in San Antonio. At eighty-seven, he's still writing. To my delight, he had a vivid memory of the Brenda Ueland incident. He was just beginning his national magazine career in 1946, and after many days of waiting in front offices, he had talked his way into a job in *Life*'s Hollywood bureau. He was determined to get an interview with the famous rodeo cowboy Bob Crosby. When Crosby didn't respond to his queries, Stanush and a *Life* photographer flew over Crosby's ranch in a helicopter, and Stanush lowered a note to him in a mason jar: "Meet me at the Maxwell Hotel." Crosby met him, and Stanush spent two weeks living with Crosby on the ranch. He filed his story at *Life* headquarters in New York, accompanied by a letter in which he described what it was like getting the story. The editors wrote back that they loved his cover letter and asked him to incorporate his personal narrative into his piece. It might have been a lesson in one of Ueland's writing classes—when Stanush was having fun telling about his experience, his story came alive. All the marks of Stanush's career as a writer and journalist are in this early profile of Bob Crosby. What Stanush excelled at, and what mattered most to him, was capturing his character's voice. For example, Crosby liked to tell about the leg he'd broken five times:

> When Crosby limped back to Roswell he told his brother, "Harold, Ah want yuh to git me the sorriest doctor yuh know." Harold said, "Ah know just the man. He ain't had a case in two years." The chosen sawbones, who was so sorry he had no office, used Crosby's kitchen as an operating room. He ripped the bad leg from knee to ankle, "an' it opened like a Bible." Then, using a pocketknife dipped in alcohol, Crosby helped him scrape the bone. When the job was done he asked the doctor how much he owed. "Think I done a nice job there," the doctor said with professional pride. "Two dollars." Gangrene appeared in the big toe a week later, so the doctor snipped off the end of the toe with a pair of sewing scissors. Crosby dispensed with surgical services when the infection recurred a second time. He simply encased his leg in an old inner tube which he packed full of cow manure, a venerable cowboy panacea. After two days of poulticing, "the red centipedes plumb disappeared." Crosby was back in competition

a few months later. Walking on crutches and with his leg in a cast, he entered and won the steer-cutting contest at Winslow, Arizona.*

Ueland copied every sentence, making only minor changes. Crosby became Jack. And the steer-cutting contest now took place in Madison Square Garden. There's a mystery here, which has always struck Claude Stanush himself as strange: why lift entire paragraphs from a 1946 *Life* magazine article, so famous it was excerpted in *Reader's Digest*, unless you actually plan to be caught?

And caught she was, in the most public way: On April 2, 1949, six weeks after her *Collier's* story appeared, the *New Yorker* published two columns under the heading "Funny Coincidence Department." On the left side were five long passages from "King of the Cowboys," and on the right, the very same words, taken from "Men's Tears." By then Claude Stanush was working in *Life's* Rockefeller Center headquarters, and his fellow *Life* writers ribbed him about the plagiarism. As he remembers it, he was more flattered than irritated: "I figured if someone wanted to steal from it, and excerpt it in the *Reader's Digest*, and make a movie from it [Nicholas Ray later made *Lusty Men* based on Stanush's story]—there must have been some value to it."

Soon after the *New Yorker* exposé appeared, an editor at *Collier's* invited Claude Stanush to a fancy lunch at Rockefeller Center. The *Collier's* editor promised he would never publish another story by Ueland. He gave Stanush a check for $1,500, saying this was what Ueland had been paid for her story. He asked Stanush to sign a quitclaim, indicating that he wouldn't pursue the magazine in court. And that was the end of it. No moral outrage, no far-flung debates about the obligations of writers, only a wry note in the *New Yorker*, followed by a gentleman's agreement. The *New Yorker* editor and writer Roger Angell recalls that the Funny Coincidence items would come in

---

* Claude Stanush, "King of the Cowboys," *Life*, May 13, 1946 (reprinted in *Reader's Digest*, August 1946); Brenda Ueland, "Men's Tears," *Collier's*, February 19, 1949.

whenever a reader or subscriber noted some "tainted duplication."
They'd appear at the bottom of a column—a newsbreak in smaller
print than the rest of the page. What a far cry from today, when a
charge of plagiarism can generate a national scandal. Angell remembered that no one gave the Funny Coincidence columns "any
more attention than a knowing laugh."

But for a freelance writer like Brenda Ueland, the attention was
far from innocuous. The *New Yorker* of the 1940s was the loftiest realm
of the magazine world, literary in the worldliest, most sophisticated
way: the home for fiction by Cheever, McCullers, Thurber—fiction
for the ages—and a place that would never have published her. And
now she was appearing in its pages for the first time, not as an author
but as the butt of a casual joke. Even the most scathing book review
couldn't have been more wounding.

The insult didn't stop there. A few years later, Ueland's plagiarism
of "King of the Cowboys" was cited by attorney Alexander Lindey in
his classic study *Plagiarism and Originality* as an example of how devastating the column-to-column comparison can be in proving plagiarism, for there is no context left to show whatever differences
remain between the two works. And so, in 1952, Brenda Ueland
entered literary history as a certified literary thief. Claude Stanush
kept a copy of Lindey's book in his garage.

But how much did the plagiarism matter to Brenda Ueland? In
the box-by-box inventory of the papers Brenda Ueland donated to the
Minnesota Historical Society, amid volumes of her personal writing,
there is no reference to any surviving correspondence or diaries
from the year 1949—the year of the *New Yorker* revelation. No mention of plagiarism, *Collier's,* the *New Yorker,* or a scandal. Only the
sense, in subsequent years, of a writer plagued with anxiety about
money and obsessed with her discipline or lack of discipline—constantly weighing and measuring herself, physically and mentally.

So I'm left to imagine her motives and emotions, writer to writer.
Plagiarism today is considered the ultimate fall from grace—it means
a failing grade for any student in the university where I teach literature. As for Ueland, in 1952 she published an essay about her family

in the *Scandinavian American Review* where she announced that she had received two grants—one from the University of Minnesota and one from the Rockefeller Foundation—to write a biography of her distinguished mother, the suffragist Clara Ueland. Although after "Men's Tears" she never published another article in an East Coast magazine, she had not been blacklisted from the world of grants.

How interesting that she turned to family, and to her mother's long political career as a champion of women's rights, after her own mistake. Her biography of Clara (published posthumously under the title *O Clouds Unfold!*), a sentimental series of sketches written in the first person, put together with whatever materials came to hand, shows Ueland's strengths and her failings as a writer. She was headstrong, charming, disorganized, and enthusiastic, without much distance from her own feelings. She submitted the manuscript to twenty publishers, and twenty publishers turned it down. She rejected an offer from a vanity press.

Ueland continued to write short pieces for several more decades—polemical pieces where she championed minor causes and underdogs, reflected on health and exercise, dramatized her habits and her self-discipline. In 1960, she published a newspaper column about the cruelty of cowboys and rodeo riders to their horses—as petulant as anything she ever wrote (and perhaps a subtle dig at the genre from which she had plagiarized). Ueland's gentle lyrical voice, the Lake Harriet voice so reminiscent of Fitzgerald, had given way to something fierce, uncompromising. In her late work, she expressed outrage or approval, she gave advice, and she gave permission. She crusaded and pontificated so much that if she had been a conventional person, it would have been intolerable. Eccentric and unpredictable, she was loveable instead.

By the 1980s, Ueland had become a local hero. Small presses started to reissue her books. Her fame grew. You can follow the Brenda Ueland revival through profiles and interviews with her in the *Minneapolis Tribune* throughout the 1980s. In 1985, her memorial service was a cultural and literary event.

◆ ◆ ◆

One of Ueland's columns, reprinted in a collection of her short pieces called *Strength to Your Sword Arm*—I don't know if it was written before or after the plagiarism—is entitled "On Making Choices." Here she tried to spell out all the layers of her personality, her post-modern self: "I seem to be sometimes my mother, sometimes my father, sometimes a whiner, a great queen, or a slob, a mother, a simpering lady or an old rip, a minister, a lion, a weasel."

Most lives are as weedy as Lake of the Isles. It's our dilemma as writers to decide what to leave in and what to leave out of our life story, and how to shape the facts about our lives. Brenda Ueland did something stupid. What's more, she did it of her own volition. Then she got caught in the most humiliating way. But she kept on writing. In her old age, even after twenty rejections of her last book, she settled into a strong, uncompromising voice. Not the voice I love best—the beautiful voice of the lakes—but a voice that grabs the reader by the sleeve and won't let go, so vivid and present it turns her essays into one-woman shows.

When I think about Brenda in her characteristic mode, walking around Lake Harriet, I can imagine several of her: One is triumphant, nose to the wind, vanquishing her old age with another mile. The other is contemplative, noting everything outside of her, feeling connected, breathing deeply. Another is anxious, driven, nose to the ground, counting her miles anxiously, walking for exertion—and to forget. Brenda Ueland was searching for what she called the True Conscience, our True Self, the very Center, because, as she wrote, "this is the only first-rate choice-making center." Maybe it takes some bad choices to be committed to good ones.

MATT BECKER

The We in the Me: Memoir as Community

* * *

WITH AN EXCERPT FROM
"Behind the Boom: Memoirs of a Gen Xer"

FROM *"Behind the Boom: Memoirs of a Gen Xer"*

Every afternoon that spring semester of 1994, I came home from classes at the University of Minnesota around noon, ate lunch, took a quick nap, and headed to the East Side St. Paul YMCA, where I worked as a teacher's assistant in the after-school child care program. The meal was always quick; I watched CNN Headline News as I ate, but the stories usually just became background noise. I was far more concerned with girls and music than current events. The headline story that second Friday of April stopped me cold:

"Kurt Cobain, lead singer and songwriter of the band Nirvana, was found dead today of an apparent suicide."

He had been a heroin addict, said CNN, and had suffered from depression. They showed an image of Nirvana from a 1992 cover of *Rolling Stone,* with Cobain wearing a tee-shirt that said "Corporate Magazines Still Suck," and I remembered that he had also been critical of himself for selling out his punk principles to a major record label. Apparently his sadness and self-loathing had become too much, and he put a shotgun in his mouth and pulled the trigger.

Pundits had anointed Cobain the spokesman of Generation X—my generation—after his song "Smells Like Teen Spirit" became a massive hit in 1991. The song was a study in juxtaposition, with music that was soft and melodic one moment, harsh and angry the next, accompanied by lyrics that expressed hope and cynicism, interest and apathy. Through these juxtapositions Cobain hinted that he was uncertain not only about who he was and where he was going, but whether he even cared enough to ponder the questions. And it was this ambivalence and indifference that were supposedly characteristic of our entire generation, and the reason we had been collectively dubbed "slackers."

As I drove to work, the deejay on the car radio was trying to make sense of Cobain's death. I had never considered him the spokesman of my generation, but I knew why people my age connected with his music and lyrics. He had turned the very insecurities that made him a slacker into art, and listening to him, we knew we were not alone with these feelings. That he survived and even thrived meant that maybe we could too. So when he decided to put a bullet in his head, what did that mean for the rest of us?

The sky was grey with clouds, and it felt like winter. I opened the window a crack, and as the earthy air rushed into my car and reminded me that it was spring, the deejay played "Smells Like Teen Spirit."

◆ ◆ ◆

The We in the Me: Memoir as Community

I was never drawn to the memoir as a reader or as a writer. It always seemed a literary genre centered on the gratuitous celebration of the self, in which authors prove to the rest of us just how extraordinary their lives have been, or how their seemingly ordinary lives are, in the end, actually extraordinary. I think I developed this attitude because I grew up in the shadow of the sixties generation.

As a member of Generation X—the cohort born between the mid-1960s and the early 1980s, and thus immediately after the post–World War II baby boom—I was a teenager and a young adult in the mid-1980s and early 1990s, the same period in which those who had been my age during the 1960s became the establishment. In their new adult positions as pundits and politicians, professors and parents, these boomers were quick to trumpet anything associated with their youth. After all, they had been inspired to political action by John F. Kennedy and Martin Luther King, Jr., and had created the Student Nonviolent Coordinating Committee and Students for a Democratic Society. They had marched in the civil rights movement and in anti–Vietnam War protests, and they had demanded greater equality for women, homosexuals, American Indians, and other oppressed communities throughout the world. The more radical of them had even sought to overthrow the entire capitalist system, which they considered the root of all inequity and militarism. They had also listened as the Beatles, Bob Dylan, Jimi Hendrix, Janis Joplin, and the Grateful

Dead—all members of their generation—redefined popular music. They had produced new fashions and lingoes, taken new types of drugs to experience unexplored states of consciousness, and even formulated new ways of relating to one another and the world. At places like San Francisco's Haight-Ashbury neighborhood and the Woodstock Music and Art Fair, they had created an entire counterculture around bell-bottoms and long hair, LSD, and *Sgt. Pepper's Lonely Hearts Club Band,* free love, togetherness, and egalitarianism. The boomers could rightfully be proud of the role that they played in the significant social and cultural changes of the 1960s. How could we Gen Xers compare? How could we come up with anything that would compete?

It's easy enough to argue against sweeping generalizations made about generational change. But those generalizations play a role in popular culture, marketing, and politics, and they can have a real impact on people's perceptions and actions. Boomers lamented that our generation was nowhere near as revolutionary, engaged, or optimistic as they had been when they were our age. Boomers "are having a heyday calling [Xers] apathetic, shiftless, causeless navel-gazers," noted a 1993 *USA Today* article.* These supposed characteristics of my generation were summed up with a single disparaging term—"slacker"—which was derived from director Richard Linklater's 1991 film of the same name, about the aimless lifestyles of underemployed and overeducated twentysomethings in Austin, Texas. We Gen Xers alternatively saw the boomers as a smug and narcissistic generation, and we were sick of their criticisms and tired of hearing about the grand experiences and accomplishments of their younger years.

Maybe I was repelled by the rise of memoir during this same time precisely because it seemed to give the sixties generation yet another way of drawing attention to its youth.

• • •

* Karen Peterson, "Baby Busters Rise above Elders' Scorn," *USA Today,* September 23, 1993. Quoted in Stephen Earl Bennett and Stephen C. Craig, eds., *After the Boom: The Politics of Generation X* (Lanham, Maryland: Rowman & Littlefield, 1997), 2–3.

Boomer nostalgia tends to override a more nuanced view of these bygone days. And because they have become the establishment and thus dominate the public discourse, the romantic vision of the 1960s frequently prevails, even if a less than glorious interpretation may be equally valid—and, indeed, was current at the time.

Examples abound. Take *The Graduate,* that iconic film of 1960s youth culture. While Ben could be understood as a countercultural character who shuns the stifling discontent of the plastic world of adulthood for a more meaningful life, he's also a young college grad without ambition who opts to coast along instead of work. He even moves in with his parents and spends his days loafing around the pool. His reckless breakup of his estranged girlfriend's wedding near the end of the film might illustrate the sixties maxim that all you need is love, but as the two flee from the church on a public bus, their faces suddenly go from smiles to blank stares. Instead of excited hope for a future of blissful togetherness, their expressions show sudden panic: "What did we just do, and where do we go from here?" Apparently, love is not all you need when you both lack direction. Or consider those youth of the 1960s who took Timothy Leary's advice to "turn on, tune in, drop out" through LSD. While the psychedelic doctor may have envisioned the drug as a tool that would eventually help those who used it transform the world, most young people instead took it to get lost in a private sensory explosion of pretty colors.* As the 1960s wore on, more and more decided to heed only the last part of his dictum and simply dropped out of society altogether, sequestering themselves in communes or religious cults, inward turns that, one might argue, set the stage for the Me Decade of the 1970s. Some may laud these sixties youths as heroic resisters of the mainstream. But they look more like slackers, to me.

In fact, in many cases, the supposedly revolutionary attitudes and actions of sixties youth culture weren't really all that different

---

* Jay Stevens, *Storming Heaven: LSD and the American Dream* (New York: Perennial Library, 1988), esp. chaps. 25, 26.

from the mainstream. The hippie's do-your-own-thing ethic, for example, was basically a variation of American rugged individualism, whereas their illicit drug use for pleasure and insight echoed a long American tradition of using narcotics and alcohol for relief and escape. The most egregious of these inconsistencies was that of the supposedly progressive young men who simultaneously criticized the submissive gender roles of the older generations, touted free love and egalitarianism, and expected women in the movement to wait on them. This glaring double standard kick-started the Women's Liberation movement.* In a 1971 issue of *Rolling Stone,* that bible of the sixties generation, music critic John Landau pondered these hypocrisies, asking, "We tell ourselves we are a counterculture. And yet are we really so different from the culture against which we rebel?"†

Of course, there were plenty of youth like Landau in the 1960s who were aware of these contradictions and worked to diminish them. Likewise, there were many who were deeply committed to so- cial justice, equality, and peace and who did not turn inward as they aged but, instead, like the late Paul Wellstone, they never stopped championing these celebrated sixties ideals. The point is to recognize that the sixties generation, like all generations, has never been monolithic in its attitudes and behaviors. As cultural historian Jay Stevens puts it in *Storming Heaven: LSD and the American Dream,* his detailed study of psychedelic drugs and sixties culture, for each young man during that era "who wanted to seize power, dismantle the Establishment, and redistribute the wealth, there were at least ten others who just wanted to get through school, get laid, get a job, and get out of going to Vietnam." For every one "who grew his hair long, smoked dope, listened to rock music, and proclaimed an urgent longing to make a clean break with American society, there was

* Sara Evans, *Personal Politics: The Roots of Women's Liberation in the Civil Rights Movement and the New Left* (New York: Alfred A. Knopf, 1979).
† Quoted in Godfrey Hodgson, *America in Our Time* (New York: Vintage Books, 1978), 326.

a corresponding kid who drank beer, worshiped the local football team, and measured his personal worth by the car he drove."*

In the same way, it's a mistake to think of Generation X as a monolith of cynical slackers whose nihilism and pessimism are outweighed only by their apathy. After all, we comprised the first significant fan base for U2, one of the most politically engaged, hopeful bands in rock 'n' roll history. And in the late 1990s, people in their early twenties volunteered 39 percent more frequently than had people that age in the mid-1970s.† Indeed, I have always suspected the motives of those who charged my generation with being cynical: was it some hippie-turned-hip-capitalist attempting to play on our insecurities in order to sell us tennis shoes? Or some civil-rights-marcher-turned-political-pundit condemning us as apathetic because we weren't championing her favorite cause?

Yet it would also be a mistake to think Gen X is without slackers, cynics, or nihilists. How else to explain a television cartoon like *South Park*, which is produced by a couple of Gen Xers and portrays *every* institution and person as corrupt? If polling data on the political views and behaviors of my generation has been correct, we have indeed been more apathetic and less hopeful than earlier generations of the twentieth century. In the 1998 congressional election, for instance, turnout among voters aged eighteen to twenty-four was less than 17 percent, roughly half that of older voters.‡ Maybe this is because, compared with the boomers, we have spent most of our lives in a historical period that has, in fact, been less promising.

• • •

* Stevens, *Storming Heaven*, 232.
† Robert Putnam, *Bowling Alone: The Collapse and Revival of American Community* (New York: Simon & Schuster, 2000), 129. Putnam suggests that these twentysomethings might belong instead to the generation following Gen X. Because of their birth years in the mid to late 1970s, however, they could also be considered late Xers.
‡ From Joan Didion, *Political Fictions* (New York: Vintage Books, 2001), 332. For more on the lower level of political engagement among American youths compared with that of older generations, see Putnam, *Bowling Alone*, 36.

Gen Xers came of age in the post-Watergate era, when belief in the integrity of official institutions had eroded considerably and damning messages about the government and its leaders became the norm. We lost faith that we could ameliorate these institutions as we witnessed the baby boomers become the very establishment that they had so passionately promised to change. Raised in an age of downward mobility that began in the 1970s (after the first wave of boomers had been educated and were launched into adulthood), we have faced an employment market increasingly characterized by rapid deindustrialization, offshoring, and outsourcing, in which traditional careers with permanent contracts and good salaries and benefits have more and more been supplanted by service industry and short-term contract "jobs" with no benefits, low wages, and little security. For much of our lives, the "facts" of the news have been filtered through political spin-doctoring or watered down with human interest stories and infotainment, while the "truth" of religion has been distorted by televangelist scandals or sexual abuse crimes. With divorce rates rising from just over 300,000 in 1965 to nearly 1.2 million by 1985, even the family and romantic relationships have seemed to us decidedly uncertain propositions.* Is it any surprise those of my generation might be a little less optimistic and trusting?

We also matured amid the excessive individualism of the Reagan era, when the president and his New Right coalition dismantled the social welfare programs associated with Roosevelt's New Deal and Johnson's Great Society because they thought them too collectivist and too expensive. Reagan and the New Right believed that the free market, not big government, could best meet society's needs and that individual success or failure was more a matter of personal responsibility than any socioeconomic issue that could be managed by bureaucrats. Such an outlook was expressed perhaps most suc-

* Divorce statistics from Peter Hanson, *The Cinema of Generation X: A Critical Study* (Jefferson, NC: McFarland & Company, 2002), 11.

cinctly by Reagan's conservative counterpart in Britain, Margaret Thatcher, who declared in 1987, "There is no such thing as society. . . . There are individual men and women and there are families and no government can do anything except through people and people look to themselves first."* This was the message our most prominent and powerful leaders stressed as my fellow Gen Xers and I came into political consciousness: that although both individualism and communalism have been central to American (and British) national identity, the former would now unequivocally come first.

The seventy-five million baby boomers, we were told, were born into an affluent post–World War II world where parents doted, schools were well funded, neighborhoods were tight knit, and Kennedy promised exciting "New Frontiers." In contrast, the fifty million of my generation were born into an era of economic stagflation when divorce and crime rates rose, budgets for schools and community centers were cut, and behind Reagan's promise of a "Morning in America" lurked punitive policies that favored the powerful and punished the vulnerable. As a generation of latch-key kids, we learned to look out for ourselves, and by the time we were old enough to protest and attend concerts, downward mobility amid triumphant free-market greed had made it harder to be concerned with the collective good.†

Besides, it didn't seem to us that all that togetherness had done much anyway, as many of the problems the sixties generation sought to change seemed even more intractable. True, the war in Vietnam had ended, but now we had a president in Reagan who spearheaded the largest peacetime military buildup in American history. Yes, Jim

---

* Douglas Keay, "Aids, Education and the Year 2000!" in *Woman's Own*, September 23, 1987, 8–10; it is reproduced on the website of the Margaret Thatcher Foundation at www.margaretthatcher.org/speeches/displaydocument.asp?docid=106689&doctype=1.
† Population numbers for boomers and Gen Xers from Bennett and Craig, *After the Boom*, 2–3. For more on the differences between the generations, see Donna Gaines, *Teenage Wasteland: Suburbia's Dead End Kids* (Chicago: University of Chicago Press, 1998), 237–61.

Crow laws were gone, but we still had Willie Horton ads, politicians complaining of welfare queens, and other slippery specters of racism. And how much did the relaxing of sexual and gender norms associated with the free love and feminism of the 1960s and 1970s have to do with AIDS and the higher divorce rates of the 1980s and 1990s?

The trend toward the individual over the community that began in the 1980s has also been encouraged during this same period by technical revolutions that have greatly facilitated the privatization of leisure. With the introduction of cable television, personal computers, the Internet, MP3 players, and similar new technologies, people are no longer beholden to the content or scheduling of the Big Three television networks, national and local print news, major record and radio companies, and other providers that dominated the media for much of the twentieth century. This shift has democratized the media, allowing us access to an unprecedented breadth and depth of information, misinformation, and entertainment whenever and wherever we want, which we can tailor to our interests and biases as never before. But this media personalization has also helped erode community, as we are no longer united by the common experience of watching the same national television news program, listening to the same regional radio station, or reading the same city newspaper. And, too often, the more immersed we become in our own media worlds, the less time we devote to daily human interaction.

In this hyperindividualistic era, community seems devalued, elusive, and perhaps even unnecessary. Maybe this is why scholars like Robert Putnam have found that people of my age are more likely than previous generations to value the personal and private over the public and collective. But this doesn't mean that we don't still long for community. Putnam, for instance, contends that unfulfilled desires for community have related directly to the rates of unhappiness, depression, and suicide among younger people that started to rise in the 1970s and 1980s.* Such self-destructiveness might be the

---

* Putnam, *Bowling Alone*, 259, 263.

ultimate testament that by nature and history humans are pack animals and that our need to interact with others of our species does not disappear, even if we seem determined to drown out this instinct under isolation headphones.

This longing for human connection amid increasing privatization and social fragmentation helps explain the celebrity-centric American media and the phenomenon of reality TV—both of which have come of age with my generation. Infotainment shows like *Entertainment Tonight*, which first aired in 1981, provide glimpses into the private lives of celebrities, suggesting that, because the famous confront the same quotidian life issues as you and I, we could get to know them on this human level. Reality TV, which began with shows like MTV's *The Real World* in the early 1990s, presents everyday people with whom viewers can easily identify, in purportedly unscripted situations (which in fact are heavily scripted) with which we can easily relate. Even local and national news programs play on this desire for a more personal connection through human interest stories.

This need for human interaction also helps explain the popularity of social networking sites like MySpace and virtual reality games like World of Warcraft, which are particularly attractive to those of Generation X and the cohort that has followed us, Generation Next.* These technologies offer a closer approximation of traditional human interaction than infotainment and reality TV because they allow users to communicate with each other via online texting or chats, enabling a give-and-take essential to face-to-face relationships. Hence my friend who frequently plays World of Warcraft considers a group of players from around the world to be genuine friends who can help him through tough times: during a recent illness, he felt obligated by

* Andrew Kohut et al., "How Young People View Their Lives, Futures, and Politics: A Portrait of 'Generation Next'" (Washington, D.C.: Pew Research Center for the People and the Press, January 9, 2007), 13–15; see http://people-press .org/reports/pdf/300.pdf.

friendship to get up, log on, and join in, whereas otherwise he might have stayed in bed all day, wallowing in his misery.

Through these virtual human connections, these various media forms seek to salve the very feelings of social fragmentation and isolation in us that they help produce. But they are ultimately unsuccessful. Because no matter how much we may relate to the celebrities on infotainment shows or the "everyday people" on reality TV, we can still only know as much about them as the producers of these programs decide to show us. Even if we could look past this lack of give-and-take, we would still be faced with the commercials, product placements, and other signs of corporate sponsorship that serve as constant reminders that the ultimate goal of these programs is revenues, and that the relationships they attempt to cultivate with us are only a means to this end. And while my friend might experience a sense of community through World of Warcraft, he has actually met only the graphical representations, or avatars, of his online friends. For all he knows, the stunning twenty-five-year-old billionaire heiress with whom he is flirting could be a sixty-five-year-old man, while the muscle-bound warrior who is helping him slay a monster could be a twelve-year-old girl. How connected can we be to someone if we're not even sure he is who he says he is? How real can a friendship be when it is formed in an entirely unreal world, where common activities involve living the virtual life of a billionaire or slaying monsters? And if he did meet a stunning heiress in person, would he still have the social skills to flirt with her for real?

Like the celebrity-centric media, reality TV, and social networking sites, books of memoir have the potential to both create and salve feelings of social fragmentation and isolation. If viewed as the gratuitous celebration of the self, the genre seems yet another example of individualism trampling community. But because a well-written memoir shows readers an individual's thoughts and emotions as the author attempts to record and make sense of his or her life, it also generates feelings of human connection. Indeed, because these self-explorations are grounded in the details of an author's lived experience, they tend to have greater depth than personal stories on TV, greater truth than relationships from social networking sites. As a result, memoir has the potential to produce in us a strong connection to the author's humanity, and it is from this connection that the genre also has the potential to build community. As memoirists record and make sense of their personal history, they demonstrate the complexities of their life, no matter how extraordinary or seemingly commonplace, how exemplary or abhorrent. By allowing us access into their private thoughts and emotions as they undergo this process, they encourage us to identify and empathize with them—two important building blocks in the creation of community. For example, although I intellectually understand the social construction of race, June Cross's memoir *Secret Daughter: A Mixed-Race Daughter and the Mother Who Gave Her Away* made me identify and empathize with a little girl as she learned from the actions of those around her that she was black, and my emotional understanding of how day-to-day interactions impose a racial identity deepened.

Of course, such identification and empathy is also possible in fiction. But memoir somehow elicits feelings of human connection that are stronger than those generated by fiction. Perhaps we are better able to recognize our own lived experiences in those of others. Or perhaps, because these stories and characters are presented as real, we accept them as real, and the feelings of connectedness seem truer. At the very least, this element of the real serves to counter an increasingly virtual world, in which it is becoming easier to falsify identity. And just as in face-to-face relationships, memoir's potential to build community is strengthened by such bonds of trust.

Given this potential, I believe that memoir may, in its own modest way, help us meet the challenges of the current historical moment. For while I think the sixties generation gets it wrong when they romanticize their own youth or question mine, they were right when they looked for solutions in togetherness. Confronted by such overwhelming challenges as global climate change, I believe that the future depends upon us thinking more about our common interests as a species and less about our uniqueness as individuals. If memoir can promote these common interests through a focus on individual uniqueness, then its celebration of the self is not gratuitous. It instead has a vital purpose.

Quite an optimistic thought from a supposed slacker...

PATRICIA HAMPL

You're History

• • •

WITH AN EXCERPT FROM
The Florist's Daughter

FROM *The Florist's Daughter*

These apparently ordinary people in our ordinary town, living faultlessly ordinary lives, and believing themselves to be ordinary, why do I persist in thinking—knowing—they weren't ordinary at all?

What's back there? Back there, I say, as if the past were a location, geographic rather than temporal, lost in the recesses of old St. Paul. And how did it become "old St. Paul," the way I habitually think of it now, as if in my lifetime the provincial Midwestern capital had lifted off the planet and become a figment of history, and from there had ceased to exist except as an invention of memory. And all the more potent for that, the way our lives become imaginary when we try most strenuously to make sense of them.

It was a world, old St. Paul. And now it's gone. But I still live in it.

Nostalgia, someone will say. A sneer accompanies the word, meaning that to be fascinated by what is gone and lost is to be easily seduced by sentiment. A shameful undertaking. But nostalgia shares the shame of the other good sins, the way lust is shameful or drink or gluttony or sloth. It doesn't belong to the desiccated sins of the soul—pride, envy. To the sweet sins of the body, add nostalgia. The sin of memory.

Nostalgia is really a kind of loyalty—also a sin when misapplied, as it so often is. But it's the engine, not the enemy, of history. It feeds on detail, the protein of accuracy. Or maybe nostalgia is a form of longing. It aches for history. In its cloudy wistfulness, nostalgia fuels the spark of significance. My place. My people.

Another old–St. Paul way of thinking: Mother talking about her people, meaning not the nation, but the clutch of family streaming back to illiterate Kilkenny, her Irish grandfather who wouldn't take up a gun during the Traverse des Sioux "Indian Uprising" (*I couldn't shoot. I played with those boys*), her mother one of "the seven beautiful Smith girls, tall as men," and their one lone brother, feebleminded, wandering the street with a small tin drum. And he the handsomest of them all. Pity, pity.

Or she would say my folks, that mild Midwestern descriptor. My people, my folks, Mother and Dad—M & D in the private patois of the fervent journals I've kept all these years as if I were doing research for a historical novel forever incomplete because the research keeps proliferating. Until now. Now the research is almost done.

◆ ◆ ◆

You're History

In May 1975, I quit a perfectly decent, if dispiriting, editorial job in St. Paul, bought myself a sky blue backpack and the cheapest transatlantic ticket I could find, and flew to London. From there, by Channel ferry and then by train, I lurched across western Europe to the Iron Curtain border town of Cheb, a cheerless crossing straight out of a Hollywood Cold War spy movie, where I finally achieved Czechoslovakia, thus reversing the late nineteenth-century journey my paternal grandparents had made when they emigrated, separately, from the Czech lands of the Hapsburg Empire to the American Midwest where they met and married in the Czech enclave of St. Paul near the Schmidt brewery.

On the Czech visa form, under the word "Profession," I had written with an impostor's bravado, "Writer." I hadn't published anything yet. Nor had I traveled before to Europe—or really, to anywhere. But that was the point: go to Prague, a certifiably exotic setting, and then write a book about it.

I did not undertake this mad Cold War leap "to find a self," as the dust jackets of so many memoirs routinely proclaim. Like legions of wandering souls of the notorious sixties bearing the hump of a backpack, I possessed more self than I knew what to do with. Though I wouldn't have put it this way at the time, I had quit my job and alarmed my mother (*you can't go behind the Iron Curtain!*) not to find a self but to find a history.

The significance of history was what my life sorely lacked. Of this I was certain. The emphasis here should be on the modifier— how *sore* I felt, had always felt, nursing the bruise of insignificance. This cultural ache is a heartland heritage, the flyover birthright. And ridiculous partly because it's inaccurate—as if there were no "history" in the migrations that brought Europeans to middle America and exiled or, as we would say today, "cleansed" its native inhabitants—to name only one strand of the midwestern story.

This moody midwestern petulance has quite a provenance. "Yours from this hell hole of life and time," Scott Fitzgerald wrote peevishly from St. Paul to Edmund Wilson, his Princeton pal in louche and literary Greenwich Village. And in a late poem John Berryman, my humanities professor at the University, evoked Minneapolis with a bilious contempt I approved—"site without history!" Even the most celebrated Minnesota novel, Sinclair Lewis's *Main Street,* was an indictment of the small-mindedness of Gopher Prairie (really Sauk Centre, Minnesota, as I was painfully aware). There it was again: the dread midwestern theme of insignificance immortalized, its author awarded the Nobel Prize for nailing us.

I knew no one in Prague, didn't have the language, and had no identity or contacts to trade on. Fine. Aware of the paradox that I was traveling to what was, after all, my ancestral homeland, I would be a stranger in a strange land.

And I was. It seemed I was the only American in Prague in spring 1975, certainly the only one staying at the Paříž, a dingy art nouveau cream cake of a hotel. If it was meant to conjure Paris, the Paříž definitely was not, in those bleak Cold War times, a figment of the city of lights. The Alfons Mucha bas-relief decorative figurines wept sooty coal dust tears, the whole place was sepulchral, the dour restaurant and lounge resembling viewing rooms of a down-market funeral parlor. I could say *pivo*—beer—and often did, and potatoes—*brambory.* Beyond that I never knew what I would be served, because the purple mimeographed menus that bled onto my hands were in Czech and Slovak, German, Russian. Rarely in French, the only foreign language I could pretend to read. Never, if memory serves, in English.

I couldn't afford regular meals at the hotel anyway, even at the funny-money prices of Cold War Prague where the dollar bill had the heft of gold bullion. I dined on angry-looking sausages at stand-up canteens and kiosks on Václavské náměstí, orange grease oozing onto the flimsy paper plate next to a chunk of damp dark bread and a knob of horseradish-laced mustard. Or I sat in smoky cafés drinking silty coffee, making a meal of caffeine and sugar. And I walked. And walked and walked. And walked some more. I was walking—I was sure—in history. I couldn't read the signs on the buildings or in the museums, I could barely pronounce the street names, sounding them out like the illiterate I was. But the history I was greedily taking in, the necessary nutrient I had been missing, comprised not only old buildings and ancient smells (those medieval wine cellars, dank with the sedge of ages). I was accosted by the raw evidence of political reality and historical destiny on the twisting streets of Malá Strana leading to the Castle. And just as I'd always suspected, if inchoately, history wasn't just a story reconstructed from the past. It wasn't quite dead and gone. And it wasn't the tame pet I had nurtured at home. History was a beast. You could feel its hot breath seething down the city's miserable byways.

History radiated from living emblems everywhere on display. Before I met or spoke to a single soul, except to say "*pivo, prosim*" to the gloomy waiters padding over the threadbare carpets of the Paříž lounge, the city impressed on me its likewise gloomy political history as I wandered its streets. Aggressively primal red-and-yellow banners sagged and flapped from the ghostly neglected buildings attesting, I learned, to fraternal relations with "our Soviet brothers." Barely six years had passed since the Warsaw Pact invasion crushed the Prague Spring attempt to develop "socialism with a human face." The faces on the streets were all too human—morose, inward, afflicted. Is it possible that I never saw a smiling face on the street then or during subsequent trips I made to Prague in the late 1970s? Gray, gray—the buildings and the faces. Absurdly, I cannot remember a sunny day either, as if the weather were in sour conspiracy with the politics, held captive by the dark side of history. But that, we know, is memory at work, that most unrepentantly poetic faculty of mind. Still, it's all I have left as a weather report from that time.

Small, almost diffident plaques punctuated the blackened walls of Malá Strana buildings, noting the place where a boy or girl—the ages always seemed to be barely twenty—had fallen, shot by the retreating Nazis in the final desperate days of the war, early May 1945, exactly thirty years before my own May visit. Most of these shrines were decorated with fresh flowers (it was lilac time, as it had been during the uprising) or bore handmade tinfoil wreaths trailing streamers in the Czech colors—the same red-white-and-blue as America's.

I stopped in front of one glass-encased photograph on Karmelitská, the clattery 22 tram rattling past me, arrested by the black-and-white face of a dead girl—I couldn't think of her as anything else. Her features were noble as a statue's. A university student probably. The lilacs tucked into the flower holder attached to her picture were fresh. Who, I wondered idly, had decorated this modest memorial?

Her parents—the thought came as a jolt. All of these private shines affixed to the grimy buildings in the disintegrating city were probably tended by elderly mothers and fathers, still grieving loyally. History was that recent, that alive.

I had been correct, back in St. Paul, to believe that history was what John Berryman called "the rudiments of a soul" that a place must achieve, usually through brutal experience, in order to matter. I had rightly rebelled against the throwaway line: *You're history,* we say to indicate you're nothing, as if "history" were a synonym for forgetfulness, worthlessness, for the absence of memory. Surely it is an American idiom. Impossible to imagine a postwar European saying, "You're history. . . . That's history," meaning fuhgeddaboudit, pal.

But history wasn't simply the glittery wash of significance I had longed for and imagined in my brooding flyover way. Until Prague, had I ever been able—or willing—to imagine its crushing reality, its indelible stain of dried blood? More to the point, having looked into the photographic face of the dead girl patriot on Karmelitská, how was I to respond to the humbling wake-up slap of historical empathy smarting on my earnest, unmarked, midwestern face?

◆ ◆ ◆

Reader, I wrote a book. Those Cold War Prague visits and my memories of growing up in a Czech American family in St Paul came together to form *A Romantic Education,* published in 1981. The adjective in the title was (or was meant to be) ironic: just how romantic should—can—a person hope to be in the face of history, either personal or public? And what *was* the relation between public and private? Between history's story and a personal account?

And what on earth was this thing I had written?

It did not occur to me—or apparently to my publisher—that I had written something called "a memoir." The word does not appear on the book jacket or in the catalogue copy. And when I was introduced to the business side of the writing life for the first time, I was dismayed when the no-nonsense sales rep hailed me by braying out, "Love your book. Don't know how to pitch it."

Pitch it? I saw the tidy lozenge of my pink and gray book sailing over home plate—a swing, a miss.

It was explained to me that a sales rep had something like thirty seconds, a minute tops, to describe a book to a bookstore buyer. *You'll love this novel about. . . . We're very excited to be publishing the definitive history of. . . .* But how to describe my book in thirty seconds? I couldn't do it myself. *The story of a young nobody traipsing around Prague, thinking about her girlhood in St. Paul and about history in "a faraway country" among "people of whom we know nothing"*—in Chamberlain's immortal description of Czechoslovakia before Munich. Czechoslovakia was still far away, even less known or cared about after almost thirty years shrouded behind the Iron Curtain than it had been when the prime minister uttered those shameful words that ushered in World War II.

At readings, I was frequently introduced as a novelist by the English professors who invited me to their campuses, my book routinely described as a novel. It told a story, it was literary—must be fiction. Autobiographical—certainly, so what else but a novel? At the time, the word "memoir" conjured up the image of a retired army general turgidly refighting old battles or an aging starlet retailing old affairs.

Or at least a life story with some kind of harrowing tale-to-tell. My book was scant on battles, empty of erotic high jinks or personal alarms. Even my dentist brother was perplexed. *What is this? You want to be a writer—sex and violence, sex and violence, Patricia.*

In bookstores, where I crept around the shelves looking to see if my book was stocked, I found it—if I found it—wherever it had been pitched, as the sales rep would say. It might turn up in Women's Studies or European History or Travel Writing. Occasionally, inexplicably, in Art History (those descriptions of art nouveau buildings, perhaps?). In stores catering to a literary clientele, it was often sequestered on a narrow shelf labeled Belles Lettres or Essays. On a good day, it might surface in Biography (my high-profile neighbors tended to be Dashiell Hammett and Jean Harlow). And one unfortunate day, there it was, consigned to the dismal precincts of Self-Help.

I would give a lot to remember when I started thinking of my book as a memoir, when I began to think of myself as a memoirist. It would not have been a happy day.

There were two strikes against autobiographical writing, in my view. One was literary and bore kinship to my brother's clarion call for "sex and violence," which I reinterpreted to mean that *real* literature must be an act of creation. You constructed, out of experience and from the mysterious depths of the imagination, characters, setting, conflict, plot—call it a novel. The great works of magisterial fiction—think *War and Peace*—were inextricably bound to history but were *better* than history precisely because they subsumed it and thrillingly embodied it. They made history come alive because they fashioned characters who lived history right before us. Such fiction gave us not only history but the meaning of history in individual lives.

My other mistrust of autobiography was more personal: I had been brought up not to talk about myself, a worthy sanction, surely.

And given my sense of being from Nowheresville, I had no impulse to protest this injunction. Besides, surely it was unfair to *use* other people—one's family, friends, people met on a train—people who were unsuspecting players in what we affectionately call real life and who were not, after all, the game subjects of journalism. And—another stumbling block—how could the first-person voice claim documentary reliability? Beyond that, who could possibly care about my life—which, in any case, was still just beginning as an adult? Hardly the time to write one's memoirs.

Stay away from all that. Write a novel. Or do your homework and write history. Or, if given to a fascination with individual lives, write biography.

I had tried.

My first intention, well before my trip to Prague, was to write a biography of my Czech grandmother—a virtual medieval peasant, classic immigrant, domestic worker in America, nonwriter of English, foreigner in our midst. She had lived a long life, to ninety. She lived near us and, later, with us, until I was out of graduate school.

Write about what you know. And did I ever know Nana.

I also felt, with the kind of burning passion that gives you the sustaining torque to write a book, that she *mattered*. She was part of history as nothing else around me was, as far as I could tell. She stood for—for what? For what I came to think of as the "lingering life of immigration." I wanted to write her biography as an act of history. She was my subject, but the theme was much larger than a single life and encompassed in my dreaming mind (the mind that caused me to quit my job and scare my mother by going to Prague) the evergreen story of American immigration, the narrative gift that keeps giving to our history and our culture.

My grandmother was dead several years when I came to all this. From childhood, I had the habit of asking her questions about her life in the Old Country, as she always called where she had come from. She never said "Bohemia." She always used the mythic term the "Old

Country," as if to underscore the absolute abyss separating her *Then*, lost in the mist of the past, from the bland *Now* she shared with me.

But before I went to Prague, as I looked at my meager notes and thought of what I remembered about her life in the Old Country, I was dismayed to see how little, how heartbreaking little, there was to tell. I had perhaps two shards from the great funeral urn of her immigrant life: a description of Christmas Eve in her village (*We walked in a procession, everyone with a candle, up to the church, a line of lights all the way up the hill, singing*) and the pathos of her favorite meal at home—a potato, mashed with milk and butter. Butter, a holiday treat.

Besides that, what was there? That her brother Rudy had been shot in the leg for poaching on the noble's estate. She said "the noble" as if this weren't a category out of gothic fiction, out of a fairy tale.

What else? That her mother had died when she was two, and her father had married a woman who did not like her. And the astonishingly gracious forgiveness of the congenitally humble: *She couldn't help it; she didn't know how to be a mother.* It was more the poverty of this maternal coldness than the poverty of the family eking out a living as farm workers in south Bohemia that apparently occasioned her flight to America. That and moxie. She left home at sixteen and never returned, the two subsequent world wars effectively cutting off all communication over time.

This is what I had to work with by way of primary sources. I managed to spin this out to something like eighty pages of text, inflating the descriptions and larding the stringy lifeline with Czech history I was reading with growing absorption. But I knew, with that inner dread of self-knowledge that won't be assuaged, that my eighty pages were dead, the prose leaden. I could barely bring myself to read the manuscript, even to try to revise it. The deletion of an adjective or the change of a comma wasn't going to bring this Lazarus text to life.

I stuffed the eighty pages in a box and put the box in my closet behind the overshoes. Maybe I couldn't write a biography. It is hard to describe the depth of disappointment I felt in acknowledging this failure to myself. I knew my grandmother was not a subject for fiction—or not for fiction I wanted to write. I had no interest in writing historical fiction. I wanted to write history. I wanted to document the great historical experience in which she was perhaps a bit player—*my* bit player. I had worked as a journalist, and I thought I knew my grandmother, my subject, and I knew how to write sentences. Wasn't that enough?

Well, no.

About a month after abandoning the project, I wrote, out of sheer loving (and frustrated) commemoration, what I suppose would best be described as a rhapsody about my grandmother's garden behind the little house near the brewery in St. Paul and another piece about her Sunday dinners, extravaganzas of her cooking and baking skills. These were each several pages long and had no particular beginning, middle, or end. They were simply patches of prose. I put them away too. But with this difference: I had a mystified awareness that these pages, unlike the diligent eighty pages hidden away with my overshoes, were alive.

This was confusing. Was I writing fiction after all? No, this was documentation, as close to a record as I could hope to muster. It was memory, of course. But hadn't my descriptions of my grandmother in the unthinkable tedium of those first eighty pages also come from memory?

It came to me, with dismay, that the difference was—me. I had conscripted myself not only as the narrator of these two little evocations but as the searching self, the need-to-know protagonist. The urgency I recognized in the prose was not my grandmother suddenly resurrected but myself allowed to exist as an inquiring mind moving over the field of her existence. My need to know, even my uncertain hunches, the very lacunae of my knowledge and of the public record of history—all these were not problems but the lifeblood of the whole enterprise, the writing of a life.

I was still writing *her* life, still writing about history, about the "lingering life of immigration," but I was not doing so as a real or hopelessly phony (those awful eighty pages!) authority, swaddled in sham objectivity. I was still committed to the truth and to what facts I could shore up. But I finally understood my job as the classic writerly one: to be an observer—not only of what I saw but of what I was thinking.

Memoir, for me, became an accumulation of images, the way a family album doesn't provide a neat story line or even the facts but a collection of moments, pictures you have to sort out, muse about, wonder at. This is what we call "a world." The job of the memoir was to make personal sense of it.

Memoir, then, was only partly the work of telling a story. It was also thinking about the meaning of the broken bits of a story constructed from looking at the unsorted snapshots, the shards left of a life. The roasted potato mashed with milk, the golden coin of butter, the singing voices in the candlelit line up a hill to the church, the shot whizzing across the noble's estate, finding its prey, the brother's shattered leg.

I saw my project as a work of historical reflection. Hence the trip to Prague. As I was to learn, autobiographical writing, which cannot pretend to have a plot like a novel, cleaves to the travelogue like a great narrative life-ring. If, as our most ancient metaphor has it, life is a journey, then a travel narrative is the natural form for a memoir. But the journey was not, for me, into the excavations of history but into the mystery of memory, its byways, its detours, its vistas. The method involved research—reading Czech history, reading other memoirs of Central Europe, the travel itself. In its even more intimate investigation of images, floating pictures, observations, and the silences of history, memoir shared the habits of lyric poetry, where the personal voice, idiosyncratic as it must be, is understood—and required—to be sovereign.

Perhaps I shouldn't ask when I realized I was writing memoir. The more useful question would be to ask when the rest of the world—reviewers, readers, libraries, and bookstores—began to call books like mine "memoirs." When did the memoir become part of the cultural landscape, a literary form whose purpose was understood not (or not entirely) as reminiscence but as a kind of contemporary quest literature, a genre of storytelling and essay writing enfolded together? A form inevitably wedded to the documentary commitment of history as well as to the psychological truths of fiction and the witness of poetry.

I can report that in 1992, when my second memoir, *Virgin Time,* was published—a book about my Catholic upbringing and an inquiry into the contemplative life that took me to Assisi to find St. Francis—bookstores routinely shelved it in Autobiography or Memoir. In the decade since I had written *A Romantic Education,* the form had sidled into the trade market neighborhood and quietly taken up prime real estate. And, as far as some critics were concerned, it began ruining literary property values.

The memoir has been, on the one hand, a startling success story in American publishing in the past quarter century. But it has also been literature's changeling, the bad apple, ever suspect, slightly illegitimate, a brassy parvenu talking too much about itself. It has never entirely overcome the taint of chronic self-absorption. And it has been caught in lies, not something the novel or even poetry need worry about.

None of this troubled me as I went about writing my first two memoirs, because in both cases I had my sights set on a subject beyond myself. My subjects were the "lingering life of immigration" and the "contemplative life." As I saw it, both of these books rose out of the life I had been dealt—Czech American and Catholic—but they weren't *about* me. They were books in which I employed myself to investigate larger subjects. Both of these books involved a lot of research, a lot of travel, years of pursuit. And a focus on the bigger picture.

And I was reading other books that were kindred, in a sense creating from my reading a private canon of memoir. I had never read a memoir in college or later in graduate school. Who studied memoir?

Who went to graduate school to write it? You went to an MFA program in creative writing to write fiction or poetry. Nonfiction belonged to journalism.

Some of the books I was discovering were long available, though perhaps little read, like Alfred Kazin's evocative postwar masterpiece *A Walker in the City*, and Czesław Miłosz's *Native Realm*, a Polish exile's Cold War memoir by turns sternly intellectual and passionately lyrical. Others were more recent, magisterial works of witness from the long Soviet night like *Hope Against Hope*, by Nadezhda Mandelstam, and Eva Hoffman's poignant *Lost in Translation*.

These writers used the autobiographical voice to penetrate dark, ignored corners of history. I could whistle my way past the literary jeers and criticisms of memoir as a form, the routine disdain, the accusations of self-absorption (and my own innate hesitations), by reminding myself of these essential works of the personal voice, spoken in the face of crushing historical reality. Talk about speaking truth to power—these were my heroes, and though my narrative position was far humbler, I honored these works above all.

"You're not writing another memoir, I hope," a celebrated novelist friend whose work I treasure said one day, as if he'd given me long enough to get over my bad habit. "When are you going to get to the real books?" Meaning, the novels. I thought, with bruised solidarity, of Leslie Fielder's (mostly admiring) review of *A Walker in the City*, in which he accused Kazin of writing a book that "perversely refuses to become a novel." I could do worse.

Then, relatively reassured about my enterprise, I wrote a book that flew in the face of my grand, rather heroically selfless claims about the memoir in the service of history. I wrote a book about being the daughter of my mother and father. A Mom and Pop book, a how-I-got-to-be-me memoir. Just the sort of memoir that is the butt of so much literary contempt, a contempt I had been willing to acquiesce to and, sometimes, even share—as long as my less self-regarding books were seen on a different plane entirely. A higher plane, of course.

The reason a writer writes a certain book and not some other book (or no book at all) is a mystery. In fact there is no reason. A book is first a project, and before that it exists as what is best called an "itch." You write the books that won't go away until they're written. It is not a choice so much as a recognition. And it often goes against the grain.

Somewhere along the years of writing those books about the "lingering life of immigration" and the "contemplative life," I realized I had another subject, which for some years (well before I wrote anything) I thought of as the "daughter book." I had no children, but I had been, deep into middle age, a daughter, living near my parents, watching them age as the inevitable role reversals played out until, finally, I was the parent and each of them, in turn, became the helpless being curled in bed beneath a blanket.

There was no travelogue format to serve as a narrative net for this book—no gallant trip behind the Iron Curtain, no hike through Umbria to Francis's flowery Assisi. My parents had lived their modest middle-class lives in the middle of the century in the middle of the country in St. Paul. They were going nowhere and so was this book.

But it also refused to go away.

I dragged my heels, thinking maybe I just wanted to write a brief elegy in prose, something too small to turn into a book, something almost unnoticeable. But the project refused to help me in this way: it wanted room. I had no idea how to shape the memories of what I came to think of as "old St. Paul," the town of my girlhood, before the freeways, before suburban sprawl. I was alarmed to think I might sink into the marshmallow crème of nostalgia. I had hated St. Paul! I was still astonished I'd never left it. How could I be nostalgic about it? Or *was* this nostalgia, this ardent, almost raw urgency to evoke that lost world as, finally, my mother was being lost to me?

I was back where I'd started with *A Romantic Education*, writing from shards and memories, taking notes as well on the last months of her life, finally the last night. With her death, perhaps as the solemn residue of a life, I hardened my purpose. And found, or was given by her death, my form.

I had written a sentence in my notebook that proved to be the book's launch, though I had actually written it in despair: *Nothing is harder to grasp than a relentlessly modest life.* My father's life, my mother's, indeed the life of my family and everyone we had known in St. Paul—modest, middling, gone now. It struck me, in the hush of grief, after they were gone, that this was a way in. More than that, this modesty was a *subject.* My father, my mother, their *world.*

The book I wrote, set on the final night of my mother's life, as I held her hand in the hospital, writing, with my other hand, her obituary for the *St. Paul Pioneer Press,* was a memoir of that modest world. *The Florist's Daughter* traveled nowhere on the globe as my other books had in my persistent search for historical meaning. The journey I made in this book was not geographic. It was entirely temporal, into history itself, the Depression that had formed my parents and deformed their hopes and dreams, the postwar life of hard work, the qualities of quiet idealism (my father) and furious political grudges (my mother), the sweep of their decades leading each of them to pure acquiescence. Theirs was the acquiescence of humble lives, lived well but without glory, as the world changed around them and left them at the side of the speedway.

This, then, was history. I had to acquiesce to it, too. I no longer had the illusion, no matter how well intentioned, that history was Out There—behind the Iron Curtain, in the dawn star of the Renaissance in Italy. It was possible—actually it was necessary—to write history from the inside if I hoped to preserve my bit of truth, put it forward on the great heap of history.

"Doubtless every family archive that perishes," Czesław Miłosz wrote in *Native Realm,* "every account book that is burned, every effacement of the past reinforces classifications and ideas at the expense of reality. Afterward, all that remains of entire centuries is a kind of popular digest. And not one of us today is immune to that contagion." He, like all my heroes of memoir, had been writing out of the same sense of worthlessness that had haunted me. I had thought they at least—Miłosz, Mandelstam, Hoffman, Kazin—had known they were writing about the great occasions of world history. Surely, with the deaths and exiles, the wars and political hauntings from evil times they had witnessed, endured, or inherited, *they* were assured the value of their enterprise in writing their lives.

But here it was again, evidence of the fragility of the homely detail, of intimate family life. This ordinariness is the fact of most of our lives. It is, paradoxically, what history strains against, in its recording of wars and migrations, glorious triumphs and traumatic changes. For this personal modesty of ordinary lives is what we mean, finally, by happiness. And happiness, it appears, is the opposite of what history usually concerns itself with.

This modesty is what must not be lost in the telling of our lives. The glory of the ordinary is an oxymoron, but ordinary life is family life, daily life, what we cherish and strive to sustain. Yet it is always lost, over and over, again and again, war by war, age by slippery age. And so to write an elegy, as I learned again with my book about my Mother and Dad, is to write history—and to write history is, inevitably, to write an elegy.

CHERI REGISTER

Memoir Matters

◆ ◆ ◆

WITH AN EXCERPT FROM
Packinghouse Daughter: A Memoir

FROM *Packinghouse Daughter: A Memoir*

In a town without museums or amusement parks, which Albert Lea still
was in the late 1950s, elementary school field trips tend to be excursions
in industrial technology. Touring the sites where people do their daily work
has to serve as both entertainment and education. My classmates and
I clucked at baby chicks still wet and sticky and confused in the electric
incubators at the hatchery, and watched a row of women at Kroger's Produce "candle" freshly laid eggs; lighting the eggs with a lamp from behind,
they could see inside and check for embryos. We crowded around the
printing press that clanked out the *Albert Lea Evening Tribune,* made our
voices echo in the tall stairwell of a grain elevator, and stood entranced
as bottles and cans moved along conveyor belts to be automatically filled
and sealed at the Morlea Dairy, the Coca-Cola bottling plant, and the National Cooperatives cannery. We never did visit the mysterious, brick-
walled Olson Manufacturing Company on South Broadway, so we could
still chime in with the local joke, "Why are there so many Olsons in Albert
Lea? They make them here."

These field trips rarely bored us. I assumed my classmates were as fascinated as I was with the notion of work and its secret words and special
skills. Mom taught me "dart" and "tuck" and "gusset" and showed me how
to use a gauge and a tracing wheel. As I helped Dad with his house projects,
I learned "dowel," "trowel," "sillcock," and "miter box." I looked forward
to the day when I would master something and speak its language with
confidence, but until then, I enjoyed peeking in on the work that grown-ups
did, and seeing who did what, and where. For the parents of us Lincoln
School kids, "where" was likely the Wilson & Co. packinghouse.

We knew that a visit to Wilson's required some degree of maturity, or
at least the early signs of adolescence. A hodge-podge of brick buildings
and tin and wooden sheds, Wilson's sat in a shallow depression between
U.S. Highway 16, our Main Street, and the Chicago-Milwaukee-St. Paul
and Pacific railroad line that ran along the weedy shore of Albert Lea Lake,
also known as Lower Lake. "The plant," we called it, a name that marked

it as the primary local industry. Security fences and a large employee parking lot made it look vast and impenetrable and even a little scary, yet it imposed itself on our lives in ways so familiar and habitual we rarely paid attention. The ceaseless industry of the packinghouse filled the air on the north side of town with a smoky, rancid odor, turned Albert Lea Lake slimy with effluents, alerted us to the passage of time with a steam whistle at noon, blared out livestock prices on our radios, and kept many of us fed and clothed and sheltered. "The Wilson label protects your table," was not only an advertising slogan, but the literal truth. We knew there would be no table to sit at if it weren't for Wilson's.

◆ ◆ ◆

Memoir Matters

In the 1990s, as memoirs like Mary Karr's *The Liars Club* and Frank McCourt's *Angela's Ashes* began to compete with novels in popularity, a few literary critics grew alarmed. James Wolcott warned in *Vanity Fair* that literature might devolve into "a big earnest blob of me-first sensibility."* Paul Gray, writing in *Time*, puzzled over "the success of unhappy stories by the largely or completely unknown."† While they could certainly cite examples to warrant their fears, the critics overlooked memoir's promise. Despite beginning with "me," both orthographically and narratively, memoir draws on shared, or public, memory as well as the strictly personal. The most fully realized memoirs situate personal memory in precise public places, the specific geographical, historical, and cultural settings where life-shaping events occur.

Overwrought confessionalism is, of course, a risk in any form of writing derived from personal experience. Without deliberate attention to context, memoir can indeed fail to convey much meaning. What would *Angela's Ashes* be without the crowded lanes of Limerick,

---

* James Wolcott, "Me, Myself, and I," *Vanity Fair*, October 1997, 214.
† Paul Gray, "Real Life Misery. Read All About It!" *Time*, April 21, 1997.

or *The Liar's Club* without the Texas Gulf Coast oil rigs? Memoirists who let their personal pinings float in a featureless nowhere, mistaking it for everywhere, misrepresent the genre, but they do not negate its value. Hokey novels, too, find their way into print yet leave the genre untainted.

The surest way for memoirists to win readers' interest and empathy is to locate their personal stories in public space. I have worked to accomplish this in my own writing, yet when I teach creative nonfiction writing, I realize how hard it can be to convey. Many of my students, creatures of American individualism, believe that their stories derive from a uniquely personal vision known as "my truth." Context is clutter, added as illustrative detail but tricky to integrate with the main story. History is an especially hard sell. Asked to write about public events that determined the course of their lives, some students come up blank, while others recount TV news stories that aroused their sympathies or opened their eyes to the plight of others. Only a few look back to determinative events before their births, as Diane Wilson has done in *Spirit Car: Journey to a Dakota Past.** She traces her family's welfare and her mother's "passing" as a white, suburban housewife to the Dakota War of 1862, which demanded painful loyalty tests of mixed-race people who had previously enjoyed access to both cultures. As the state of Minnesota celebrates its sesquicentennial and reencounters this troubling moment in its past, the personal witness offered in Wilson's memoir can enrich the public discussion.

Sometimes a lesson about the importance of context arises naturally in class yet takes an offensive form. A student of color who reads to the class from work-in-progress might hear, as peer criticism, that he should make clear from the start that he is Korean or Ojibwe. Otherwise, how will readers know? Yet the student offering the advice has not owned up anywhere in her text to being white or Methodist

* Diane Wilson, *Spirit Car: Journey to a Dakota Past* (St. Paul: Borealis Books, 2006).

or a native of Illinois soybean country. To shortcut this class dynamic, I like to assign an excerpt from John Edgar Wideman's *Fatheralong*, plucked out of the text in such a way that it places his child self squarely in Pittsburgh without immediately identifying him as African American, unless the reader knows the city neighborhoods and bus routes. White students sometimes tell me they have to adjust their image of the narrator when they realize he is black. Without evidence to the contrary, they assume a white norm, and finding themselves suddenly face-to-face with someone else is unnerving. This gives us a chance to talk about the double standard applied to "mainstream" and "marginal" memoirists. As readers, we justly expect a clear view of the person narrating the memoir, yet as writers, we who imagine ourselves as mainstream easily forget to say who and whose we are, where we come from, which places, events, and cultures have shaped us, and how.

Maybe the Korean or Ojibwe student will plant a jar of kimchi or a bit of beadwork in the story as a quick—and stereotypical—signal to the reader. The white student might confess to being middle class. The Catholic student might cite first communion jitters about fumbling the host or describe the slap of an ornery nun's ruler. But it is not enough just to peg ourselves. These clues have become too hackneyed to carry any news, and sometimes such hints obscure the truth. Whenever I identify my upbringing as Scandinavian Lutheran, in a Minnesota town of less than twenty thousand, I risk drowning in the deluge that Garrison Keillor's Lake Wobegon has become. The memoirist's task is to complicate the oversimplified, to rescue truth from the truisms that readers adopt as shorthand for lives they see only from a distance, comic or otherwise.

Description alone won't rectify misperceptions. I learned this lesson years ago, backwards, in a personal essay class taught by Phillip Lopate in his term as visiting creative nonfiction mentor at the Loft Literary Center in Minneapolis. He had spoken encouraging words about the first essay I submitted for class critique, so I sprang to attention when he announced that my second essay had left him cold. In an attempt at lyricism, not my natural mode, I had written an elegiac piece about my love-hate relationship with cornfields, and I had pulled out all the sensory stops to awe the reader with corn. Lopate confessed that he just didn't get it. There was nothing at stake in my essay for a reader not already obsessed, let alone unfamiliar, with cornfields. Moreover, he admitted, as a native of Manhattan, he didn't really get the Midwest or midwestern writers' reverie about prairies. I showed the essay to Minnesota writer Paul Gruchow, who wrote brilliantly of prairies, and he gave me one of the best pieces of writing advice I've received: Remember that you come from an exotic landscape. You are introducing your landscape to a reader who can't even imagine it.

Cornfields, exotic? Yes, as much in need of careful, accurate, astonishing representation as the surface of Mars.

During the darkest days of winter, I like to ask my students to spend a chunk of class time—maybe fifteen minutes—writing something that will make winter vivid to a reader from the tropics. Both native Minnesotans and newcomers go right for the sensory detail: the prickly touch of an icy wind on the cheek, the crunch and ping as the ice scraper battles the frosty windshield, the sound the snow makes underfoot at varying temperatures, the stark beauty of light and shadow in mid-December, the bright Arctic blue sky on a sub-zero January day. They write with precision and passion, and once they have taken their turns reading aloud, we feel reinvigorated, ready to head back out into the cold.

I take weather seriously. I grew up in southern Minnesota's Blizzard Belt, known in the summer as Tornado Alley. When the prominent feature of your childhood landscape is a huge sky of ever-shifting moods, you learn that human resourcefulness is no match for nature, even if human folly and greed are altering its age-old patterns. A quick spatter of sticky snow on a windshield, a skid through a red light, or a tree limb cracking under the weight of the snow can mean sudden death. My learned respect for the Upper Midwest's climate, and thus for uncontrollable turns of fate, shows, I believe, in my writing. A colleague from the urban East once called my take on life "passive." I call it "responsive."

In the years since my conversation with Paul Gruchow, I've expanded his advice and passed it on: We all come from exotic landscapes. We all live in dramatic times. We are all raised in inscrutable cultures. For uninitiated readers to get it, we have to push beyond description to interpretation. Here is what my place in the world looks and feels like, here is what happens there, and here is how it shapes my vision and my encounter with life.

When I make that shift in my own work, I arrive at testimony, which is where my voice feels most authentic. My particular vocation as a writer is to bear witness to what I know because of where and when I am living. I home in on experiences I share with some others but that most people don't understand or may even misperceive. Still the blizzard-bound girl, I am alert to the dangers lurking within beauty—the injustice in the happily-ever-after story of international adoption, for example,* and the beauty that is danger's reward—the clarity and purpose in a life of chronic illness.† The witness says: I bring you vital news; here is what I know that I want you to understand.

The most useful testimony is often counterintuitive. Rather than confirming readers' assumptions about the lives that others lead, memoir ought to shake them up. D. J. Waldie's *Holy Land: A Suburban Memoir* certainly freed me from my skewed view of suburbs as transitory, trumped-up places. Waldie has described his writing on greater Los Angeles as a counternarrative meant to undo the film noir version of LA as an ugly, menacing city where dreams are dashed for evil

---

* Cheri Register, *"Are Those Kids Yours?": American Families with Children Adopted from Other Countries* (New York: Free Press, 1991) and *Beyond Good Intentions: A Mother Reflects on Raising Internationally Adopted Children* (St. Paul: Yeong & Yeong Book Company, 2005).
† *Living with Chronic Illness: Days of Patience and Passion* (New York: Free Press, 1987; Bantam Books, 1989) and *The Chronic Illness Experience: Embracing the Imperfect Life* (Center City, MN: Hazelden Publications, 1997).

gains. My current work, using memoir, family history, and the public record to examine perceptions of Minnesota, tosses me up against a similar cynicism. The story favored on public television, abetted by certain academic historians, depicts the rural Midwest as a de-populating wasteland.* It reduces Minnesota's 150-year history since European settlement to a relentless trajectory of ruin. Lumbering denuded the forests. Agriculture uprooted the prairie and drained its wetlands. The railroads spawned towns too close together to survive and abandoned some of them outright. Decline set in on day one. Although it is true, the story doesn't account for the lives and dreams of the people who settled in Minnesota. At any one moment in this century and a half, you find plenty of hope to counter the over-riding narrative's despair.

I found, as I began to write, that I must test the resonance of this public story against what rings true personally. I grew up in this doomed landscape, the great-great-granddaughter of territorial pioneers and the granddaughter of Danish immigrants. They came neither to destroy the land nor to submit to the hardships of a crass, exploitive plundering of resources. My paternal ancestors were populists who believed that human society could be progressively improved. Their 1893 train trip from Moscow, Minnesota, to Chicago for the World's Columbian Exposition likely confirmed their vision.†
My maternal grandmother, a boardinghouse kitchen servant in Denmark, toiled over a hot stove as the proprietor of a small-town beer joint–café in America. On her first visit to Denmark forty-seven years after her emigration, she bought a set of Royal Copenhagen

---

* *Minnesota: A History of the Land,* documentary, University of Minnesota College of Natural Resources and Twin Cities Public Television, 2005; Joseph A. Amato and John W. Meyer, *The Decline of Rural Minnesota* (Marshall, MN: Crossings Press, 1993); Richard O. Davies, David R. Pichaske, Joseph A. Amato, eds., introduction to *A Place Called Home: Writings on the Midwestern Small Town* (St. Paul: Borealis Books, 2003).
† My knowledge of this trip comes not from family lore but from the public record, a county newspaper—an argument for using public documents to write memoir.

china as proof of her good fortune. Never mind that the dishes were factory discards. I own a share of them now, and I cherish their imperfections. The lens of decline would focus on the Registers' financial failures and the alcoholism in the Petersen family to squeeze them into the currently fashionable template. Yet both families taught me to hope, to work, to laugh, and to tell stories, even in the face of gloom.

Packinghouse Daughter, my childhood memoir, came into being as a counternarrative. The prevailing images of the rural Midwest and of the American working class seemed discordant and didn't suit my life within them. I heard the Midwest described as stodgy, conservative, homogeneous, impervious to new ideas, resistant to social change. The American working class consisted of urban, ethnic industrial workers with a radical grasp on social ills, eager to strike and bring on the revolution. The first image seemed an insulting caricature; the second, a romantic fantasy. They were mutually exclusive, besides. There could be no such working class in that rural Midwest. Yet I knew myself to be a midwestern working-class girl. Both those attributes were so central to my identity and to my family history that I had to make better sense of them than any existing narrative could.

Telling "my truth" was no simple task. At one of many moments of frustration, I handed my writing group— a remnant of Phillip Lopate's class—a long, shapeless draft. They advised me to write two separate books: one, my personal memoir, and the other, a book about labor and the meatpacking industry. I mulled their advice for several days, and although it was off the mark, it worked wonders. I realized that without the meatpacking story, I had little to say about myself that would hold even my own interest. Without my personal stake in the subject, a book about packinghouse labor would be dry and unmoving. I felt no passion or motive to write either book. A firm conviction set in that my memoir would matter only if I wrote it at the intersection of private life and public history. I've been parked on that corner ever since.

Writing about working-class life also set me at odds with the dominant story of American democracy. "Class" is that nasty set of divisions the British adhere to, a hierarchy we Americans discarded in the Revolution. We have our rich and our poor at the extremes, and in between, a boundless middle class where most Americans, even many of the rich and poor, locate themselves. To describe and interpret working-class life, I first had to testify to its existence. The pretense that the United States is a classless society, or so fluid that everyone but the most abject failure surges upward, left me with no suitable vocabulary. Marxist rhetoric proved a poor fit. There is no consensus in American discourse about the meaning of the word "class" or about the conditions that determine who fits where. Yet even with no clear meaning, the very word "class" is potent and threatening. Democratic election campaigns have adopted the term "working families" to appeal to the party's traditional labor base without feeding their Republican opponents' charge that they are encouraging "class warfare."

Meanwhile, the class structure in the United States is shifting and throwing the terms out of sync. College students assigned to read *Packinghouse Daughter* wonder why I use "working class" to describe families who own houses and cars. They equate the term with the "working poor," and they are right. Families like mine, with hopes of mobility sustained by steady employment at union wages, are nearing extinction. My story misleads unless I allude to the reorganization of the meatpacking industry, the faster-paced and lower-paid work, the diminished strength of the unions, and the replacement of stable blue-collar communities with a mostly immigrant workforce that turns over frequently. While my personal story might be read as a typically American journey upward,* the public story in

* *Packinghouse Daughter* was published with only one typographical error. The designer accomplished a last-minute change in the font used for "UPWA," the abbreviation for the United Packinghouse Workers of America, my dad's union, with a quick find-and-change-all operation. Thus I am described in the text as "UPWArdly mobile," a turn of fortune for which the UPWA certainly deserves credit.

Packinghouse Daughter fits the narrative of relentless decline. Cynicism lurks in its margins. Where should the reader look for hope? Odd though it may seem, I take comfort in D. J. Waldie's assertion that "every American place is a ruined paradise." If we already know that to be true, we are no longer compelled to keep telling the story. Like the spate of memoirs about family dysfunction, dirges about the loss of the American dream no longer bear news. Memoirists and historians both are free to ask, So what? And now what?

Memoir, drawing on intimate, subjective experience, can deepen and complicate these dire public histories we acknowledge as true. Bill Holm's essay "The Music of Failure" assumes we know the story of midwestern decline, then pokes at our acquiescence in it by showing us the Icelandic immigrant Bardal family—failures by all common measures—whose tiny, cramped house contains a massive library. "That house," he writes, "was a metaphor for the interior life that they stocked with the greatest beauty and intelligence they understood." Holm republished the essay in a memoir titled to make its message and its setting clear: *The Heart Can Be Filled Anywhere on Earth: Minneota, Minnesota.*

I learned in an immigration history class how eagerly the second generation discards Old Country habits in order to become totally American. I still cheer the day I encountered Maxine Hong Kingston's *The Woman Warrior: Memoirs of a Girlhood Among Ghosts,* which showed me how fraught the vaunted assimilation process is with struggle and sorrow and poignant comedy and that it demands constant cross-cultural negotiation. Kingston's Chinese American narrator helped me understand my Danish American mother, who refused to teach me the Danish language because it was ugly and useless. When I kept begging, she relented with two sentences: *Jeg strøg idag. Jeg skal stryge i morgen.* ("I ironed today. I will iron tomorrow." The story of her life?) Years later, however, when I studied Danish on my own, she was pleased. My requests for vocabulary and idioms and correct pronunciations opened doors that had slammed shut in my ornery adolescence. I also learned that my family spoke an outdated lower-class dialect. Toward the end of her life, after Alzheimer's had stolen her speech, I imagined that her mind had regressed to her childhood language. I spoke to her in Danish, and she laughed heartily.

The Woman Warrior was useful to me because I read it not as a private, exotic, Chinese story, but as a public, American one. Kingston, through her astute depiction of place, time, and culture, of a public context, had given me both options. Usefulness is, for me, a measure of a memoir's value. I want my memoir, as well as those I read, to matter, to make some difference in the world. Personal accounts do have the capacity to inspire, and readers are drawn to the survival stories of people who have overcome illness, addiction, or abuse. Yet memoir has a greater capacity: to transform.

When I think of memoir as testimony, it is precisely this transformative end I have in mind. Testimony that is only self-revealing can be distancing and divisive. Given context, an examination of the public places that shape the experience revealed, it can help reconcile. A case in point is the personal literature on international adoption, a realm of experience that I have written about myself. A narrative of destitution and rescue and happy endings dominated the storytelling in the 1960s and 1970s. As rising infertility in Western industrial countries became the primary motive for adopting, the story changed to one of mutual need and fated love.* A counternarrative has emerged in the last few years as a large population of primarily Korean adoptees has reached adulthood and begun to write personal accounts—some book-length memoirs,† but also essays and poems that draw on memory.‡ The story they tell is about abandonment, loss, grief, uncomprehending adoptive parents, confused

* Accounts by adoptive parents have been standard fare in *Adoptive Families* magazine since it began publication (as *OURS Magazine*) in 1968.
† For example, see Katy Robinson, *A Single Square Picture* (New York: Berkley Books, 2002) and Jane Jeong Trenka, *The Language of Blood* (St. Paul: Borealis Books, 2003).
‡ These are found in anthologies, including, for example, Tonya Bishoff and Jo Rankin, eds., *Seeds from a Silent Tree: An Anthology by Korean Adoptees* (Glendale, CA: Pandal Press, 1997) and Susan Soon-Keum Cox, ed., *Voices from*

racial identity, and complicated searches for birth family. Some tell that story with lyrical grace. Others slip into angry rants. It is a true story, propelled by genuine feelings, yet it puts adoptive parents and adoption agency personnel on the defensive. Some even refuse to read.

I have tried to introduce a different parental voice into the conversation that is neither the righteous rescuer nor the lucky, blessed mom of the standard narratives. While I write as an adoptive parent, I acknowledge the truth of the adoptee memoirs and interpret them in a way that I hope will encourage parents to listen. Only when we understand what is at stake for our children will we speak truthfully on our own behalf. I curtailed my attempt at a full-blown memoir, however, out of reluctance to expose my daughters' privacy. I would like to find a voice that can speak of my own sorrows and hopes and vulnerabilities so distinctly that my daughters' identities become immaterial. In the meantime, I write in a collective "we parents" voice that of course has limited validity. I look forward to a new paradigm in adoptive parents' stories: a shift of focus from the cute, little objects of the quest to the parents' deepest longings for family happiness.*

To become a transformative, reconciling force, the testimony of both adoptees and parents needs a public dimension. The adoptee memoirs tend to be highly personal, the story of "me," often cast as victim. Assembled in an anthology, they acquire the force of group witness, but similarity is their only context. The parents' stories are often glossy and naïve and treat international adoption as little more

---

Another Place: A Collection of Works from a Generation Born in Korea and Adopted to Other Countries (St. Paul: Yeong & Yong Book Company, 1999). Jane Jeong Trenka, Julia Chinyere Oparah, and Sun Yung Shin, eds., *Outsiders Within: Writing on Transracial Adoption* (Cambridge, MA: South End Press, 2006) includes essays that explore the context of adoption, as well as personal stories, and covers both domestic and international adoption.
* A recent turn toward more candor is seen, for example, in Terra Trevor, *Pushing Up the Sky: A Mother's Story* (El Dorado Hills, CA: Korean-American Adoptee Adoptive Family Network, 2006) and Theresa Reid, *Two Little Girls: A Memoir of Adoption* (New York: Berkley Books, 2006).

than a reproductive choice. I believe that a scrupulous examination of place—and international adoption is certainly an exotic place to inhabit—can lift the testimony out of the mire of hurt and shame. I await a memoir that takes care to set its story, whether of happy endings, perpetual sorrow, or lifelong negotiation, in a specific historical, geographical, and cultural space. Such a memoir might allude, for example, to social upheaval and sexual stigma in Korea and to rising infertility in the United States, to Korea's rapid emergence from wartime destruction to high-tech modernity and to expanding globalization and multiculturalism in the United States, to Confucianism's reverence for patrilineal bloodlines and to American individualism's view of children as entitlement and source of fulfillment.

International adoption is a complicated, paradoxical story, and it grows more so as its setting moves from Korea to Colombia to Russia to China to Ethiopia on one end and from Australia to Sweden to the Netherlands to France on the other. The meaning that just one thoughtful, reflective adoptee or adoptive parent can draw from life at this busy intersection of private and public might bring hope and reconciliation to others caught up in a confusing and often disturbing story. Not sociology, not economic history, not psychological research, but memoir, I believe, will deliver the news that matters most.

Delivering news is the point. Memoir introduces us readers to someone we may not know, but unless it also tells us something we could not imagine without the author's testimony, we may not care. Decades ago I wrote a manuscript about my experience of chronic illness and sent it out, unsolicited, to publishers. It was my variant of the standard strength-in-adversity story, enriched, I thought, with self-ironic wit. One of the rejections read, "Maybe if you were somebody famous this would be interesting." I was insulted. Was voyeurism the only motive for reading a personal account of illness? What about compassion, understanding, new knowledge? Later I was grateful for that rejection, and the others, as well. I would be embarrassed if that manuscript were available in print. Instead I had to start over and move beyond my private suffering toward shared space. Flannery O'Connor described sickness as "a place where there's no company, where nobody can follow," but I found it well populated with others who felt as solitary and silenced as I had. I interviewed some of them about their experience with chronic illness and found emotional, social, and spiritual commonalities that my narrow inward gaze would never have revealed. Also, their trust in me left me with a new obligation, to dig deeper and be more truthful about my own life. I had to discover the news before I could tell it. And *that* story, it turned out, *was* interesting enough to publish, even coming from an unknown source.

Discovering the news is on my mind now, as I think about what's next in my writing life. Testimony begins in obsession: Why does this topic or moment intrigue me? What can it possibly mean? My dad was a storyteller, and many of his stories were set on the farm in Moscow Township where he spent his first eleven years, the farm his great-grandparents had bought with a preemption claim in 1855 and that his parents lost in a farm recession. Turtle Creek, which ran through the farm just yards from the house, was a frequent site of his stories. He told me several times what happened when Rice Lake, a large marsh nearby, was drained into the Cedar River: how the dredge came along and reamed out Turtle Creek, how the water came flowing through so fast that the men scooped out fish with shovels and threw them onto the back of a truck. The stories were vivid memories. Much later, with a bit of research, I learned that Rice Lake was drained before my dad was born. He never knew Turtle Creek in its natural state. He never saw that truckload of fish. Yet his stories had the passion of testimony, and I believe they still bear witness to something important: Loss? Longing? Environmental destruction? Collective memory rooted in family and place? Since my dad's death, I have become obsessed with the draining of Rice Lake. I never knew it as anything but a strikingly flat stretch of farmland, yet I know that something about that event, that place, and that time—the first decade of the twentieth century—still matters. Documents pertaining to the story have fallen into my hands. There is something I might testify about, some transformation I am invited to help achieve. I don't know yet what the news will be, but the vehicle is likely to be memoir. My work is to enter that historical and geographical space to watch and listen. Unless a much easier project comes along and lures me away, you'll find me there, under an uncertain sky.

CARLOS EIRE

Where Falsehoods Dissolve:
Memory as History

• • •

WITH AN EXCERPT FROM
Waiting for Snow in Havana: Confessions of a Cuban Boy

from *Waiting for Snow in Havana: Confessions of a Cuban Boy*

The world changed while I slept, and much to my surprise, no one had consulted me. That's how it would always be from that day forward. Of course, that's the way it had been all along. I just didn't know it until that morning. Surprise upon surprise: some good, some evil, most somewhere in between. And always without my consent.

I was barely eight years old, and I had spent hours dreaming of childish things, as children do. My father, who vividly remembered his prior incarnation as King Louis xvi of France, probably dreamt of costume balls, mobs, and guillotines. My mother, who had a memory of having been Marie Antoinette, couldn't have shared in his dreams. Maybe she dreamt of hibiscus blossoms and fine silk. Maybe she dreamt of angels, as she always encouraged me to do. "*Sueña con los angelitos,*" she would say: Dream of little angels. The fact that they were little meant they were too cute to be fallen angels.

Devils can never be cute.

The tropical sun knifed through the gaps in the wooden shutters, as always, extending in narrow shafts of light above my bed, revealing entire galaxies of swirling dust specks. I stared at the dust, as always, rapt. I don't remember getting out of bed. But I do remember walking into my parents' bedroom. Their shutters were open and the room was flooded with light. As always, my father was putting on his trousers over his shoes. He always put on his socks and shoes first, and then his trousers. For years I tried to duplicate that nearly magical feat, with little success. The cuffs of my pants would always get stuck on my shoes and no amount of tugging could free them. More that once I risked an eternity in hell and spit out swear words. I had no idea that if your pants are baggy enough, you can slide them over anything, even snowshoes.

As he slid his baggy trousers over his brown wingtip shoes, effortlessly, Louis xvi broke the news to me: "Batista is gone. He flew out of Havana early this morning. It looks like the rebels have won."

"You lie," I said.

"No, I swear, it's true," he replied.

Marie Antoinette, my mother, assured me it was true as she applied lipstick, seated at her vanity table. It was a beautiful piece of mahogany furniture with three mirrors: one flat against the wall and two on either side of that, hinged so that their angles could be changed at will. I used to turn the sided mirrors so they would face each other and create infinite regressions of one another. Sometimes I would peer in and plunge into infinity.

"You'd better stay indoors today," my mother said. "God knows what could happen. Don't even stick your head out the door." Maybe she, too, had dreamt of guillotines after all? Or maybe it was just sensible, motherly advice. Perhaps she knew that the heads of the elites don't usually fare well on the street when revolutions triumph, not even when the heads belong to children.

◆ ◆ ◆

Where Falsehoods Dissolve: Memory as History

Memory is the most potent truth.
Show me history untouched by memories and you show me lies.
Show me lies not based on memories, and you show me the worst lies of all.

So I say in the preamble to *Waiting for Snow in Havana,* a book I never intended to publish as a memoir. Never. I wrote it as a novel and sold it as a novel. It said so—*A Novel,* right under the title, on the cover page of the manuscript purchased by the Free Press, in large, bold type. I wrote an account of my own childhood, straight from memory, and tried to pass it off as fiction. But my editor unmasked me early in the editing process.

She asked, point-blank: "How much of this is your own life story?"

"All of it," I admitted, grudgingly.

I wanted to lie but couldn't bring myself to do it, thanks to my Catholic schooling and my fear of hell, which has intensified as I get ever closer to my own death. Trying to pass off one's life story as fiction is not lying, exactly, but denying the ruse certainly is.

"Then we can't publish this as fiction," my editor said.

I was doomed. I had already used my advance royalties to pay off my MasterCard debt. I had no way of backing out. Now the whole world—including all my colleagues and students—would know my innermost secrets. How could I, a historian of late medieval and early modern Europe, ever write or teach again?

But thank God for my editor's insistence. As I was to discover, this meant that my memories would become history, rather than fiction. Memory is the most eloquent and persuasive witness in history. Nothing connects us to the past more directly. Memory is also our very identity, the whole sum of our being. Lose your memory and you lose yourself. Memory is more than that, too. It is the only means we have of transcending time and space, our only ticket out of the evanescent present, our deepest connection to the divine and eternal.

This is no new insight, of course. St. Augustine of Hippo knew it sixteen centuries ago. In his *Confessions*, written in the year 397, in a world vastly different from ours, he had this to say about memory:

> There I find heaven and earth, sea and whatever I can think on . . . there also I meet myself, and recall myself, what, when, or where I did a thing, and how I was affected when I did it. . . . Great is this power of memory, exceeding great, O my God—an inner chamber vast and boundless! . . . Astonishment seizes me!*

Astonishment, yes, I agree. Few things astonish me more than returning to a place where I once lived, years ago, and squaring my memories with what I see in the here and now. It happened to me recently in Minneapolis.

There I was, near the University of Minnesota in Dinkytown, and there it was, the Varsity Theater. Suddenly, the twenty-six years that

* *Confessions* 10.8.

stood between the building and my memory imploded. Same place, different time, much older man. I used to drive a hundred miles to the Varsity, just to see the films that never made it to St. Cloud, where I taught between 1979 and 1981. I'm thrown off balance by what I see. The Varsity is no longer a movie house. Video cassettes, digital video disks, and multiplex theaters have killed the Varsity I knew and loved. I slip noiselessly through the gap between past and present and find myself in the audience once again, inside the Varsity. Suddenly it's 1980, and I'm watching a movie about beatniks. John Heard is playing the role of Jack Kerouac in the film *Heart Beat*, and he is carrying around a large scroll of paper on which he is typing *On the Road*, writing in a continuous flow. His 120-foot-long autobiographical novel, an oddity worthy of Ripley's Believe-It-Or-Not, will define a whole generation. I vow to write the same way some day, on a giant roll of paper towels or some such scroll. I harbor no illusions about defining a generation but simply itch to do the scroll thing, to write in one continuous flow, from memory.

In an instant, I'm somewhere else again, nineteen years later, or seven years ago, depending on which way you count. It's late April 2000. I begin typing on my scroll, fulfilling my vow. It's not a roll of paper towels, but rather a computer screen, on which I can write continuously. I'm in my study in Connecticut, above the garage. I've decided to write a novel about a boy who lives through the Cuban Revolution and is sent to the United States as one of fourteen thousand children airlifted out of Cuba without their families by Operation Pedro Pan. I have to do it. I need to set the record straight. I have to bear witness, to speak out against those who constantly distort and deny my own history.

They are everywhere, these deniers of all the horrors and holocausts of history, including mine, and they are unavoidable. Their voices show up most frequently in the news media, drowning out all others. Even worse, I can't help but run into them all the time on university campuses, for the majority of my colleagues tend to

believe that Fidel Castro is an idealist who has done great things for
his people. Some of them are even my best friends. This may sound
odd to anyone who doesn't inhabit the academic ivory tower, but if you
doubt me, simply stroll down to any large college or university bookstore and peruse the section where the books on Cuba are shelved.
Chances are that eight or nine out of every ten books on that shelf
will sing the praises of the so-called Revolution and overlook all of
its horrors. For my entire adult life, I've had to listen to absolute non-
sense about my own past. I've put up with the worst sort of igno-
rance—ironically—among the most learned folk in the Western
world. And I've been subjected to their accusations. It's been enough
to make me hide my nationality, to stress that my grandparents were
Spanish, not Cuban. Enough to make me wish for a different name,
one that won't identify me as a Hispanic: perhaps something like
Jacques Clouseau, McKinley Morganfield, or Ludwig Feuerbach. I'm
on the very edge of sanity, perched over an abyss, driven there by all
those who have constantly denied my memories, falsified my history, and accused me of being a selfish lout:

You simply didn't want to share your stuff with the poor. You bastard.
Everything you say about Cuba is a lie. You son of a bitch.

Numbers don't matter. It makes no difference whether I hear this
from tens of thousands or only a handful of people. Every time I encounter a believer in this Big Lie, I feel the same pain, the same terror. The mere fact that *anyone* could think of Fidel Castro's dictator-
ship as a good thing—even just one person on earth—is torture, and
too frightening. If anyone can be so easily fooled, or if anyone can
willingly overlook the worst of atrocities, what hope is there for the
world? If thousands or millions can believe the Big Lie about Cuba,
then they can believe just about anything, including the absolute necessity of Final Solutions.

I can't take it any more. Elián Gonzalez pushes me off the edge.

The hypocrites in Havana clamor for the boy to be returned. His
mother has drowned at sea, like thousands of others, trying to escape

a totalitarian nightmare. The boy is now in the United States, but his father remains in Cuba, and the high priests in Havana proclaim that every child deserves to be with his father—the very same high priests who strove to keep me and over ten thousand children away from our parents, and succeeded. The very same caste who made my mother and thousands of others wait for many years before reuniting with their children. The very same oligarchs who kept thousands of us Cuban children from reuniting with our fathers. The very same comrades who prevented me from attending my father's funeral.

I write to the American news media on my Yale stationery and inscribe my august title under my signature. I ask the journalists to focus on the larger picture, please, and to cover the history of the airlift and of the unsparing efforts the Cuban authorities have made over the years to tear families apart. I mention the labor camps where fathers and mothers were sent to work as slaves for long stretches of time, away from their spouses and children—labor camps where parents were forced to spend months and years paying off their "debt" to the so-called Revolution, toiling without compensation in the tropical sun, under brutal conditions, hundreds of miles from their families. I point out that any parents who wanted to leave Cuba with their kids would be subjected to this forced separation. I make mention of the thousands of parents who are still routinely denied the right to emigrate with their children or to be reunited with them abroad.

No one acknowledges my letters.

The Cable News Network simply refers to Elián as "Cuban Boy." No name is needed under his photo. He is only a Cuban, after all, and just a boy.

And he is forcibly returned to the hell his mother tried to free him from.

I plunge off the edge and free fall.

I stop reading newspapers and magazines. I stop watching television or listening to the radio. I don't want to know what will happen to the boy. He is already screwed, no matter what. Ten times over.

Just like his fellow countrymen, all eleven million of us, whom he embodies: all Cubans everywhere, both on the island and abroad.

I write every night for the next four months, continuously. I begin writing at 10:00 P.M. every night and write until 2:00, 3:00, or 4:00 A.M. Some nights I write until sunrise, the pale gray light reminding me that I've lost track of time. I go to work early in the morning to teach my summer-term class, From Crusade to Enlightenment. In the afternoon I assume the role of department chair. When I get home in the late afternoon, I turn into dad and husband, and I eat dinner, and then, once I've done that, I read to my children what I wrote the previous night, put them to bed, and begin writing again. I do this every day, seven days a week.

At the end of four months, in late August, I have a book. And I can scroll from the first to the last page, through one continuous computer document.

My scroll. My novel.

It's a frightfully honest and accurate rendering from memory of my own childhood. Everyone has different names, of course. I've given myself a much better name than I have in real life. I've become Jesús Rubio—"Blond Jesus" in English. My nickname is very Cuban. I am Chucho—Chucho Rubio—"Blond Light Switch" in English. And the title for the book is perfect, even though it will later be discarded by my editor: *Kiss the Lizard, Jesus*.

I've written straight from memory. No outline. No rewriting either. I simply move forward with the narrative, on a scroll, guided by images. I'm possessed by my own ghost, by my memory, by the urge to tell my story, to get it out there. The story of a Cuban Boy, like Elián.

I set memory loose and pit it against the Big Lie.

And my memories crash against the Lie like an acid tsunami, dissolving its tissues, making them sputter, hiss, and smoke, turning them into noxious vapors. Memory is like photographic evidence in a courtroom: a snapshot that can't be easily dismissed. All acts of cruelty, all repression and injustice are captured by memory in its deepest recesses, and when these images are released to the world at large, they reveal very clearly the cost of something as monstrous as the Cuban Revolution. My memories, freely shared, allow readers to get into my Cuban skin. The memories vanquish all abstractions, and all statistics too. And those who praise the Revolution are thus forced to confront their prejudices toward the so-called Third World, to recognize their condescending acceptance of evil, especially of those tyrannies that masquerade as humanitarian causes.

Evil has a way of extending itself, way beyond its immediate manifestations.

My colleague Miroslav Volf has argued in *The End of Memory* that evil can triumph over and over again whenever an unjust act is erased, distorted, or eclipsed by a lie. When an evil deed is wiped clean from memory, or from history, evil wins out, and it becomes easier for the evil to repeat itself. This is where memory enters the picture as an ethical imperative. Memory is the most eloquent witness against injustice. Elie Wiesel never tires of saying this: to bear witness against injustice is to wage war on evil.

Do not deny what happened. Never again. Not in my presence. I know better.

The Big Lie comes in different versions, but it is always the same at heart. Forget the Nazi Holocaust, Stalin's Gulag, the Armenian genocide, Mao's Cultural Revolution, the killing fields of the Khmer Rouge, the presence of slaves at Mount Vernon and Monticello, the massacre at Wounded Knee. Forget each and every one of these horrors. They didn't happen, or don't really matter. Great things were accomplished.

The Cuban version of the Big Lie has its own peculiar insidious features. Without exception, the Lie highlights the "fact" that Cubans enjoy free universal health care and education. The Lie loves statistics too, which it twists with abandon. So the more one tries to expose the Lie by dwelling on the "facts" and statistics it generates, the deeper one sinks into some sort of quicksand. One can try to explain the price Cubans pay for these ostensibly "free" services or to point out how hollow their much-vaunted success is, but it will make no difference. The Lie depends on a value system, on certain myths, and on ideological constructs. In many ways, the Lie depends on something akin to religious belief. And everyone knows that beliefs that rely on myths are hard to dislodge. Those who believe the Lie will instantly doubt anything that calls their myths into question, for "facts" and statistics are always open to interpretation, especially when ideologies are exposed. Even worse, "facts" and statistics are boring. Start jabbering about such things, and chances are most readers and audiences will yawn or fall asleep.

So, never mind that in Cuba there is no freedom of speech or expression or assembly. Or that the press is run by the government and all dissent is stifled. Never mind that the health care is abysmally poor and that the so-called free education involves forced labor camps for children. Never mind that 20 percent of the population is in exile. Never mind that tourists in Cuba have access to all of the things Cubans lack and that the tourist hotels, restaurants, stores, and beaches are all off-limits to Cubans. Forget that kind of apartheid. It doesn't count. One can't even call it "apartheid" without being chastised: "How dare you!" It's the gestalt that counts: the overall shape, configuration, and political orientation of a society. Forget the details, along with the "facts" and statistics.

According to the Lie, the Revolution has been good for Cubans because they live in a Third World country, and people in the Third World don't really need something as abstract as what we call "freedom" or "human rights." In fact, the Lie goes further, proposing that "human rights" is a relative, subjective concept and that real "human rights" for Cuba and the whole Third World is simply a matter of providing adequate nutrition, schooling, and health care. It doesn't matter how they get their food, doctors, and teachers, or how inferior and awful it may all be, or how much repression is needed to make it happen, or how many lies are told. The end always justifies the means in the Third World, where the descendants of Rousseau's noble savage continue to suffer from a congenital handicap of sorts, a trait common to all who live in balmy climes and have dark complexions. They can't make progress without some Mussolini figure who will make the trains run on time, so to speak. They are so inferior, a dictator is the best they can hope for. Dictators are good for them. They can even be heroic or saintly, like Fidel.

Fortunately, I stumbled upon the best weapon I could use to unmask the Lie: my memory. It was all I had, really, so I had no choice. But its effectiveness was not dulled by chance. No one can deny the injustices visited upon me and my family by the Cuban Revolution; no one can deny the fact of my pain, confirmed in my memories. And the same goes for other authors who bear witness to the history they have lived through. I also lucked out in another way. Since my memories were those of a child, I had found within myself the perfect instrument, the most powerful of weapons against repression of any sort: the child's voice.

Do you seek proof that what we call "human rights" is more than an abstract concept? Proof of the fact that all humans yearn for a certain measure of freedom, respect, and love?

Let a child tell you about it.

Get the reader into the child's skin. Help the reader to become a child again, to relive the wonder and the fear, to laugh and weep, and to remember what it was like when the future was wide open and all emotions flowed seamlessly into one another. Help the reader to live as a Cuban in the only way that a non-Cuban could conceivably understand. Turn the reader into a Cuban Boy.

Nothing links all human beings on earth more closely than childhood. Those early years of life have a certain sameness around the globe, regardless of cultural differences. Childhood transcends boundaries, ignoring the wide gap that adults perceive between themselves and those who are "others." If you take adults back to childhood, you take them back to the core of their souls, to that part of their being where they can most readily perceive what they share with all other human beings. Above all, you can erase boundaries and remind people of their deepest longings. If you can get a reader to identify with you, to live your life as a child, the reader might actually see the Big Lie for what it is, subliminally, from within.

So, as I go into a free fall that summer—and the feeling of falling is very real and inescapable—I relive my childhood, with all of my senses on high alert. Suddenly, I see things again, hear them, touch them, smell them, feel them. My entire self is overwhelmed by images, especially. Not false images, mind you. Not idols. Sacred images, the most sacred of all: my memories.

My memories of what happened, and the intermingling of good and evil: memories of all the highs and lows, of all of what was wondrous and horrendous, of all of the love showered on me and all of the injustices I have witnessed.

Every day, several times a day, I am transported to Havana. I hear my father's voice; I hear him tell me of previous incarnations. I am scratched by stubble on his cheeks as he hugs me; I learn of my cousin being shot to death by a firing squad. I see my brother hurling rotten breadfruit at me and smell and taste it as it slams into my chest; I am told that my uncle has been whisked away to prison in the middle of the night. I hear the street vendors, their songs echoing as loudly as ever; I listen to the government informants murmuring next door. I am overwhelmed by a crimson sun sinking into the turquoise sea and by the tropical breeze on my skin; I bristle at the tears streaming down my grandfather's cheeks on that awful day when the Revolution seizes all of his life's savings, turning him into a pauper. I say farewell to my father, over and over, several times a day. And I cringe every time the militia men at the Havana airport strip me down to my underpants.

An expert on memory who once attended one of my talks told me that the most important memories all of us have are those that affect our emotions. She also said that the deepest and most important part of our memory is that which remembers injustices, and that we all have a moral compass of sorts that allows us to know when we've been wronged. According to her, psychologists tend to agree on this one point: memories of wrongs endured are the ones that shape us most intensely.

My memories and my child's voice wrestle with the Big Lie. And they also expose some of the most basic traits shared by all human beings. And as I try to expose the Big Lie and allow my memories to overwhelm me, I tap a part of my own brain that I had never used before and didn't even know existed. I also bind and gag the professor within me. And he shuts up without a struggle, happily. Instead of explaining, dissecting, and analyzing everything, I simply rely on images as conveyed by words. I discover the power of poetry through the images in my memory. I find a mantra to guide me: show, don't tell; show, don't tell.

Ironically, as I silence the professor, I also become a better historian. A historian of my own past and of my people's past. I bear witness to a shared injustice and a vanished world denied by the Big Lie. So the very same professor who had written several books before, but never, ever received a thank-you for his work, begins to receive hundreds, then thousands of thank-yous. Readers of every kind, on every continent but Antarctica, write to me, and the overwhelming majority thank me for my narrative, the non-Cuban readers saying, "thank you for telling *your* story," the Cubans saying, "thank you for telling *my* story." Big difference. Not "*your* story" or "*our* story" but "*my* story."

My readers let me know that there is more than one way to do history, that a poetic approach to the past written from memory draws the reader into other worlds more immediately and intensely. I've tapped into the truth, much more convincingly than I ever thought possible. Don't get me wrong: I'm not saying that writing from memory is superior to doing research in an archive or that historians should give up on research altogether. Not at all. If that were the case, I'd be out of a job. I'm simply saying that there are different ways to write about the past and that the first-person narrative packs a wallop of its own. By focusing on images in my memory, I can bring the reader into the world I experienced, with an emotional dimension of the sort that professional historians are trained to avoid like the plague. Relying on memory rather than documents and employing emotionally charged images rather than footnotes, I can re-create the Cuba I knew for readers in different cultures and at the same time for many Cuban readers, including those who would love to silence me.

So, since my words bear witness to a history they've been trying to erase for over forty years, the enlightened Cuban despots ban my book and proclaim me an enemy of the Revolution.

I am thrilled by this, the ultimate honor. But it also makes me weep.

I ask myself: what next?

What now, Herr Professor Doktor?

Once again, my memory allows me to monkey with space and time. I am on the Left Bank of the Seine, in one of those Parisian restaurants where the waiters outnumber the customers. A conference has brought me here. Earlier in the day I had presented a paper on a subject very few people on earth care about: the translation of devotional texts in the fifteenth and sixteenth centuries. It was a good paper, I thought. We conference participants are enjoying our banquet, thanks to our great patron, the European Union. Suddenly, someone very impolitely mentions that I had won the National Book Award in the United States. The conversation stops. Stunned silence. You could hear a pin drop or some diner slurp his soup in a far corner of the room. Everyone stares at me. The inevitable question leaps from someone's throat, like a toad: "What book?" I mention my memoir and briefly describe it, feeling great embarrassment and shame. A historian is not supposed to write about his own past or that of his people, much less to do it as if it were a novel. I have betrayed my guild.

One colleague breaks the silence and says with a very pained look on his face: "Oh . . . Oh. . . . you know what this means, don't you? It means you'll be remembered for *that* book, not for your work as a historian."

"I can live with that," I reply.

Then the French historian who is hosting the conference, a man whose work I admire, chimes in as only a French scholar can, with great precision, consummate clarity, and brutal candor: "Well . . . ," he says in thickly accented English. "Well . . . you certainly won't win a prize for the paper you gave us today."

Ouch.

So there I was, and here I am. I have strayed from my calling and, in the process, set an impossibly high bar for myself to clear—at least as far as most of my colleagues see it. Can I also win a prize for a book based on archival research? Can I atone for the sin of writing without footnotes? Probably not, many say. I have crossed a line that is taboo for most historians, though more by accident than by design: I have touched the lives of thousands of readers and produced a historical document. I have become a historical figure. I have irked a despotic regime and earned its censure. I no longer merely create useful footnotes but have instead become a footnote in the work of other historians.

In the meantime, however, no one can stop my mind from shuttling back and forth between Minneapolis and Havana and Paris, or Wolfenbüttel, or Xochimilco, or Yale, or Zagreb, or any other place on earth where I've been, during any time when I've been conscious.

Memory is the most potent truth, I still affirm. And it becomes even more potent when its treasures are examined with a novelist's eye. As I also said in my preamble:

> We improve when we become fiction,
> each and every one of us,
> and when the past becomes a novel our memories are sharpened.

So, it's back to Paris once again, back to that conference.

We're taking a break from our meeting, walking from one building to another, led by our Parisian host, the eminent historian. It's early in the morning, and I've just walked into the holy of holies for all historians of Europe: the editorial offices of the journal *Annales*, which defines the cutting edge for my profession.

It's a shockingly small office for such an influential journal and totally devoid of character. Everything is made of metal and plastic in this inner sanctum, and the windows are clear plateglass. It could pass for an insurance agency in downtown Kokomo. I expected something much larger, more imposing. Where are the Corinthian columns? The carved woodwork? The stained-glass windows? I expected some sort of tabernacle, too, where the key to the past would be enshrined. But all I can see is past issues of *Annales* on the shelves, and they look exactly like all the others I have seen and used in American libraries.

Fool. *Imbécile.*

History needs no temples, no trappings, no tabernacle. And it has many keys, not just one. We historians hold most of the keys to the past, as locksmiths at the ultimate museum, and our keys unlock doors to different dimensions, all of which are nestled one within the other, like Russian *matryoshka* dolls. But at the very center, at the deepest and most fundamental level of all—where all falsehoods dissolve like slugs in salt—access to the past is in everyone's hands. And the key to that dimension is easy enough to find. So easy, in fact, that every despot fumes at the thought of it: that key is in every memory, in the images we carry with us, and the imagination with which we approach them.

I should have known that.

SAMUEL G. FREEDMAN

Making Memory

. . .

WITH AN EXCERPT FROM
Who She Was: My Search for My Mother's Life

FROM *Who She Was: My Search for My Mother's Life*

On a windswept, darkening afternoon in December 2000, I brushed the snow away from the marker of my mother's grave. With each sweep of my gloved hand, the raised lettering of the simple plaque gradually became visible, showing her name, ELEANOR FREEDMAN, and the inscription our family had chose: A SPECIAL PERSON. It had taken me some time to find the marker, even with a map from the cemetery office and a computer print-out designating the exact location like the block-and-lot number in a sub-urban subdivision. I had not visited the grave in twenty-six years, since another December afternoon, when my family buried her.

I could still see, after so many years, the tears sliding out of my father's unblinking eyes. I could still hear my sister's howls of grief. But my memories of my mother herself had grown vaguer and less distinct over time. I could not remember the timbre of her voice or the pattern of her inflections. I could not summon her face without a photograph. What I did recall in all its shameful detail was the only visit she made to me at college, and my command that she sit rows apart from me in my classes, that we pretend to be strangers until we were safely blocks away from the classroom building. I was just eighteen then, two months into my fresh-man year a thousand miles from home, and in the full thrall of this new independence. She was already dying of cancer, pulling me back in love and obligation to the excruciating spectacle of her demise. From that day until this one, my memory of her illness, of our family's deathwatch, had eclipsed all the other memories of her existence.

Now I was forty-five, the same age my mother had been when the doc-tor found that first lump in her breast. I was only five years younger than she had been at her death. I was more than a decade into my marriage, as she had been in hers. I was the father of two children who looked at me, as I looked at her, only as a parent, not someone with a whole autonomous life, most of which had preceded their arrival. And, as if my own wish dur-ing college were taking revenge on me, I had discovered that my mother was more and more a stranger to me. Besides having been someone who died miserably and died young, I did not know who she was. . . .

An odd thing had happened, though, during the previous few months. In conversations and occasional speeches, I found myself mentioning stray details from my mother's life—her pride when Bess Meyerson was the first Jew chosen as Miss America, her dancing in the streets when the United Nations voted statehood for Israel. I wasn't even aware at first of how often I was telling these stories until an old friend pointed it out. "I've known you twenty years," he said one night. "This is the first time I've ever heard you talk about your mother." His words jolted me. I had to ponder what my reflex to speak of her meant. I carried that mystery with me from place to place over the weeks, and eventually I came to an answer. I realized that, at last, I wanted to discover my mother's life. I wanted, almost literally, to claw at that frozen cemetery ground, to exhume the soil flecked with her residue, and from it conjure the past.

◆ ◆ ◆

Making Memory

On a Tuesday night in November 1974, I arrived home from college for the Thanksgiving weekend. I had made the nine-hundred-mile drive from Wisconsin to New Jersey out of a sense of fierce, awful obligation. My mother was nearing the end of her five year struggle against cancer, and our family was now recognizing annual events as final rites.

Still, my mother insisted in her indomitable way that she cook a holiday dinner for two dozen members of our extended family. My father's best estimate was that she had several more months to live, and we had already planned to spend Christmas week in the Caribbean, a last family vacation to parallel our last family Thanksgiving. My father made his living designing and manufacturing equipment used in cancer research, and so I had no reason to doubt his prognosis.

On the Saturday afternoon of Thanksgiving weekend, then, I headed off to Interstate 80 and ultimately to Madison. I knew my mother was scheduled to enter a hospital two days later to have pleural fluid drained from her lungs. My father had reassured me this would be a routine procedure and there was no reason for me to stay home and miss classes, especially so close to final exams.

I ran directly into an unseasonable blizzard on my way west and wound up snowbound in Ohio. I finally walked into my dorm room at dusk on Monday. The note I found from my roommate, explaining that I should call home immediately, led to a houseguest's voice giving me a phone number in New York, which turned out to be at a hospital. My father answered. He told me that a medical resident had botched the lung tap and my mother was dead.

Almost thirty years later, I learned something else about the events of that Thanksgiving week. My father had bought my mother a present, something from the cutting edge of audio technology: a cassette tape recorder. He also bought her several ninety-minute cassettes. His plan, which became hers as well, was that she would dictate into those tapes her life story or her parting advice or some kind of farewell, something other than the helpless cry she loosed in the hospital: "I'm dying. My God, I'm dying."

Because my mother died earlier than expected, she never had the chance to speak a syllable into those tapes. When my father told me in 2004 about their existence, I felt both harrowed and redeemed. I felt harrowed because of all the things I had missed about my mother, perhaps the most acute was the sound of her voice. Yet I felt redeemed because by this time I was nearly done with researching and writing the story of my mother's life as a teenager and a young woman, which would be published in 2005 as the book *Who She Was*. In a very real way, I had put down on paper the words she might have intoned onto tape.

So the concept of "making memory" exists for me in a very concrete way, a process measurable in the notebooks and file folders and yellowing snapshots that built up in my office during my three years of work on the book. I had to make memory—or, to put it more accurately, to assemble memory—because memory did not exist. I was not alive during the years of my mother's coming-of-age, the years from her first day of high school in 1938 until her wedding day to my father in 1953. I was not even the custodian of second-hand memory, because my mother had shared relatively little of her past with me. And I, a typically narcissistic teenaged boy, had never asked very much about it, either. I had to retrieve the past before I could play the mental trick of convincing myself that I remembered the past.

The mission of doing so, and the meaning of that mission, puts me in mind, of all things, of a theological distinction between Judaism and Christianity. One of Jesus's most penetrating critiques of Jewish religion was that it emphasized, indeed privileged, doing over feeling. The practice of Judaism was based on adherence to 613 commandments, the *mitzvot,* that are enumerated in the Torah. For Jesus and his followers, the emotional connection to God was more important, more genuinely religious, than the fidelity to a list of requirements.

From that fork in the road derive two distinct religions that provide parallels for two approaches to memoir and family history. In our present literary climate, as in emergent Christianity, emotion is equated with truth. Factuality, much less historiography, is seen as an impediment to truth, the annoying clutter of empty ritual. Since individual memory is subjective, the implicit line of reasoning goes, then it is irrelevant to try to reconcile memory to historical evidence or even to use such evidence to fill in the gaps of memory. The unsurprising outcome of this belief system, I would say, is the number of memoirs that have been unmasked and wholly or partly fabricated, James Frey primary among them.

Perhaps because of my training as a journalist, I vigorously dispute the idea that the intellectual act of research is unimportant in memoir and does not serve art. And as an observant Jew, I have lived this truth another way. Even in Jesus's time, and certainly now, many religious Jews would say that in following the *mitzvot* they come to approach the Divine. The act enables the emotion. The tangible enables the mysterious. Or so the process seemed to me as I worked on *Who She Was*.

What, after all, could I remember, if I had no memories? How could I imagine my way into experiences so foreign from my own? Growing up in suburban affluence in the postwar decades, what kind of vicarious leap could I make into my mother's life as a child during the Depression, a teenager during World War II, a young woman finding out that her European relatives had been killed, every one, in the Holocaust? What kind of arrogance would it betray for me to think I could understand the obstacles for a tenement girl going to college or the transgressive power of a Jew falling in love with an Italian Catholic?

Regarding my mother's life across the chasm of incomprehension, I sometimes recalled an acting class I had observed in the 1980s, when I was covering theater for the *New York Times*. The class was led by Stella Adler, one of the most prominent disciples of Constantin Stanislavski, creator of the Method. Method acting is generally understood to mean a performer drawing into his or her own psyche to create a character, and in the hands of instructors such as Lee Strasberg and actors like Marlon Brando, that was certainly the case. Adler, however, embodied a different line of descent from Stanislavski. On the day I watched her, she was teaching her students how to portray royalty. And there was no possible way, she brusquely informed them, that they as members of a modern capitalist democracy could intuit the manner of a king or queen. They had no parallel experience. Instead, she showed the class slides of thrones, bejeweled crowns, the gardens at Versailles. Her liberating lesson was that you could study your way, research your way, learn your way into the role.

Which brings me back to the *mitzvot*. I could only access my mother—I could only channel my mother—by immersing myself into all the obtainable detail of her life and times. These details, far from imprisoning me in a grid of dreary factuality, provided the means for making the imaginative, dare I say artistic, leap into her soul. So often during my years of work on *Who She Was*, I envisioned my brain divided, with one part doing the cerebral chores of locating witnesses and discovering documents while the other part was reacting viscerally to my findings.

Let me explain with a single example: my mother's college transcript. One might think of an academic record as just so much data. To me, it was a decoding ring. The transcript told me that my mother had spent eight years earning her degree. That she had transferred twice in the process, once from Brooklyn College to City College's coed downtown campus and the second time from the day division into the night school. That she had majored in business administration. That she had earned mostly Bs and a number of Cs.

Most interestingly of all, the transcript carried two handwritten notations. One identified my mother as the recipient of a New York State scholarship in January 1941, at the time she graduated from high school. The other, dated two years later, indicated the scholarship had been revoked.

Until I gazed upon this transcript, I knew little of my mother's college career, and that only because I had heard it through my father. The version he had gathered from my mother and passed along to me was that she had attended college on a scholarship and had graduated magna cum laude. Such achievements appeared plausible enough, given that my mother had been the valedictorian of her high school. My sister had somehow inherited the medal to prove it.

The college transcript revealed that my mother had lied about her college record, had plodded slowly to commencement, a long way from cum laude. It revealed that, for some reason, she had set aside her academic passions—Latin, French, math, journalism—to take a more utilitarian course of study. And as for those notations, they led me to an archivist for New York State. From his records I determined that my mother had lost the scholarship because, when she switched into night school, she could not squeeze in enough credits each semester to qualify as a full-time student.

Which brought me to another question and another set of documents. The question was why she would have left Brooklyn—the best public, coed liberal-arts school in the city as of 1941—for City downtown, and why she would then have left the day session for the night division. The documents were the Social Security records for my mother and my grandfather, which I requisitioned from a federal archive. In those printouts, I could track where each worked and how much each made for every three-month interval. They showed how, as my grandfather failed even in the late stages of the Depression to find regular work, my mother took on ever more responsibility. By age eighteen she was the chief breadwinner for her family, and earning that bread meant shunting college to the nighttime hours and choosing a major that promised employment rather than enlightenment.

As I put all this information together in my brain, I felt the effects in my heart. I understood the experience of a daughter, at once dutiful and resentful, having to defer her own dreams. I never could have conjured those emotions out of my life. I grew up in the easy assurance I would attend college. I graduated in four years, endowed by my father. I worked part-time jobs only to give myself spending cash. I supported my household by little more than taking out the garbage, and I often needed to be reminded to do that.

But typed letters and handwritten notes on decades-old paper stirred in me the necessary empathy. And this process was repeated countless times in my three years of working on the book. An aluminum bracelet spoke of the marriage proposal from her first boyfriend that my mother turned down. A letter from a friend to that friend's fiancée in the navy brought me into a workplace conversation, including my mother, about how the Germans should be punished for the Holocaust. A docket of court papers unveiled the demise of her first, failed marriage.

I do not mean to make it sound like the revelations came readily. Documents conversed with other documents. Snapshots meshed with other snapshots. I often went out to interview my mother's friends and relatives and coworkers carrying the materials I had unearthed, using those artifacts to stir memory and not infrequently to help correct fallible memory.

Several critics took *Who She Was* to task for being "too factual" and thought me hopelessly naïve for writing that "facts can lead to truth." At the risk of sounding like the stereotypically embittered author who remembers every bad review, I must confess that their attacks angered and depressed me. Not for a second did they lead me, however, to doubt my methodology, my entire approach to family history. Had I wanted to invent a life for my mother, I would have written a novel. And someday, I hope, I will move into fiction. But as an act of reclamation and reconciliation, as a way of reaching beyond the grave, I needed to *make* memory from stubborn, recalcitrant reality.

ANDRÉ ACIMAN

Rue Delta

◆ ◆ ◆

WITH AN EXCERPT FROM
Out of Egypt: A Memoir

FROM *Out of Egypt: A Memoir*

I left the piazza and returned to the station and for the first time that day made out the hollow sound of water lapping against the city. Soon after, an almost empty vaporetto arrived. Once inside, I made for the stern deck and sat on the rounded wooden bench along the fantail. Then the engine gave a churn, and a boatman released the knot. As soon as we began moving, I put both legs up on my bench, the way schoolboys ride the open-air deck on trams in Alexandria, staring at that vast expanse of night around me and at the gleaming silver-jade sweeps trailing in our wake in the middle of the Canal Grande as we cut our way deeper into the night, gliding quietly along the walls of the ancient arsenal like a spy boat that had turned off its engines or pulled in its oars. Up ahead, scattered light posts studding the lagoon tipped their heads above sea level, while the moonless city drifted behind me as I caught the fading outline of Punta della Dogana and further off the dimmed tower of San Marco looming in the late night haze. Roused by the searching beam of our vaporetto, splendid Venetian palaces suddenly rose from their slumber, one by one, lifting themselves out of the night like shades in Dante's hell eager to converse with the living, displaying their gleaming arches and arabesques and their glazed brocade of casements for a few glowing instants, only then to slip back into darkness and resume their owl-like stupor once our boat had passed.

After San Zaccaria, the vaporetto took a wide, swooping turn and headed across the lagoon toward the Lido, the boat doubling its speed, chugging away loudly, with a cool wind fanning our faces, easing the thick scirocco weather, as I reclined and threw my head back. So we've seen Venice, I thought, mimicking my grandfather's humor as I turned and watched the city sink into timeless night, thinking of Flora and all the cities and all the beaches and all the summers I too had known in my life, and of all those who had loved summer long before I came, and of those I had loved and ceased to care for and forgot to mourn and now wished were here with me in one home, one street, one city, one world.

Tomorrow, first thing, I would go to the beach.

Rue Delta

After celebrating what was to be our last Passover seder in Egypt four decades ago, I remember watching all the adults in my family leave the dining table, make their way through a long corridor, and reach the dimly lit family room. There, as happened each year, everyone sat quietly, listened to music, played cards, and invariably put everything aside when it was finally time for the nightly news broadcast on Radio Monte Carlo. I never liked Passover, but this year's, our last in Egypt, was different, so I sat and watched the adults. When it was time for them to converge on the radio, I came up to my parents and told them I wanted to go out for a walk. I knew they were always reluctant to let their fourteen-year-old boy roam the neighborhood streets alone by night, but this was my last time, and the walk was to be, without my knowing it, perhaps, my own version of an aimless, farewell stroll when you find yourself walking not just to see things for the last time or to take mental snapshots for the benefit of what Wordsworth would have called the "after years," but to get a sense of how something as intimately familiar as Rue Delta, with its noises and odors and busy crowds and the sound of surf thudding nearby, could, in less than twenty-four hours, after having watched me grow up, cease forever to exist. It would be like taking a last, hopeless look at someone who is about to die or to become a stranger but whose hand still lingers—warmly—in ours. We try to imagine how we'll live and who we'll be without them; we try to foresee the worst; we look around for tiny reminders whose unsettling reappearance in future years could so easily jolt us with unexpected longing and sorrow. We learn to nip memory, like a bad weed, before it spreads. All along, though, we are no less puzzled by the loss, which cannot sink in yet, than we'll be, decades later, when we land on the same street and feel that coming back doesn't sink in either. No wonder Ulysses was asleep when the Phaiakians put him down on his native soil. Leaving, like coming back, is a numbing experience. Memory itself is a form of numbness;

it cheats the senses. You feel neither sorrow nor joy. You feel that you're feeling nothing.

After walking out of our building, I automatically headed toward the coast road, known as the corniche of Alexandria, which used to be very poorly lit in those years, partly because not all streetlights worked, but also because President Nasser wished to foster a wartime atmosphere that kept his countrymen forever fearful of a sudden Israeli air raid. There was always, during those evenings in the midsixties, a suggestion of an unintended, bungled blackout, which, far from bolstering morale, simply betrayed Egypt's rapid decline. People always stole street lamps and pothole covers; seldom did anyone bother to replace them. The city simply grew darker and dingier.

But nighttime in Alexandria, during the month-long feast of Ramadan when devout Muslims fast until sundown every day, is a feast for the senses, and as I walked past the throng and stalls along the scantly lighted street, I was, as all European-Egyptians of my generation will always remember, accosted by wonderful odors of sweetened foods that not only were begging me to grasp how much I was losing in losing Alexandria but, in their overpowering, primitive fragrance, trailed with them a strange sense of exhilaration born from the presage that, finally, on leaving Egypt, I would never have to smell these earthy smells again, or be reminded that I had once been stranded in what was for so many of my generation a blighted backdrop of Europe. I was, as always during those final days of 1965, at once apprehensive, eager, and reluctant to leave; I would much rather have been granted an eternal reprieve—staying indefinitely provided I knew I'd be leaving soon.

This, after all, was precisely how we "lived" Egypt in those days, not just by anticipating a future in Europe that became ever more desirable the more we postponed it, but by longing for a European Alexandria that no longer really existed in Egypt and whose passing we were every day desperately eager to avert.

In Europe, however, I found that I longed to go back to an Egypt from which I had longed to get out. But I did not want to be back in Egypt; I simply wanted to be there longing for Europe again.

Pascal says somewhere that virtues are sometimes seldom more than a balancing act between two totally opposing vices. Similarly, the present is an arbitrary fulcrum in time, a moment delicately poised between two infinities, where dreams of the future and the longing to return find themselves strangely reversed. What we ultimately remember is not the past but ourselves in the past imagining the future. And, frequently, what we look forward to is not the future but the past restored.

Similarly, it is not the things we long for that we love; it is longing itself—just as it is not what we remember but remembrance we love. A good portion of my life at my computer in New York City today is spent dreaming of a life to come. What should my real memories be one day but of my computer screen and its tapestry of dreams? Europeans in Egypt spent so much time thirsting for happiness beyond Egypt that, in retrospect now, some of that longed-for happiness must have rubbed off and scented our life in Egypt, casting a happy film over days we always knew we'd sooner die than be asked to relive. The Egypt I craved to return to was not the one I knew, or couldn't wait to flee, but the one where I learned to invent being somewhere else, someone else.

Every reader of my memoir *Out of Egypt* comes face-to-face with a disturbing paradox when I reveal that my Passover night walk comes not in one but in two versions—and that both, in fact, have been published. In the first version, which appeared in *Commentary* in May 1990, an Arab vendor sells me a falafel sandwich just as I reach the coast road; in the second, published in my memoir in 1995, the vendor hands me a Ramadan pastry and refuses to take any money for it.

In both versions, I stare out at the night sea and nurse the same thoughts vis-à-vis an Alexandria I'm already starting to miss. There is a significant difference, however, between the two versions. In the book, I stand alone. In the magazine, I am walking not by myself but in the company of my brother. Indeed, since I was a rather shy, indecisive boy, it was my younger brother, by far the more daring and enterprising of us two, who was more likely to have come up with the idea of taking such a walk on our last night in Egypt. The notion of eating leavened bread or sweet cakes on the first night of Passover could only have been his, never mine, though I was the atheist, not he.

My brother had a bold, impish side to him. People used to say that "he loved things" and that "he knew how to go after them." I didn't even know what they meant when they said such things. I was never sure I loved anything, much less how to go after it. I envied him.

He liked to get to the beach early enough so as not to "miss the sun," the way he liked to eat food while "it was still hot." The sun gave me migraines, and as for warm food, I preferred fruit, nuts, and cheeses. I squirreled my food; he delected in it. He liked meats and tangy sauces, dressings, stews, herbs, and spices. I knew of only one spice, oregano, because I would sprinkle it on my steaks to kill the taste of meat.

My brother would kneel before a basil bush and say he liked the smell of basil. I had never smelled basil until he pointed it out to me. Then I learned to like basil, the way I learned to like people only after he had befriended them first, or to mimic them after watching him ape their features, or to second-guess people by watching how he read their minds and said they were liars.

My brother liked to go out; I liked to stay in. On clear summer days, I liked nothing more than to sit on our balcony at the beach house and write or draw in the shade, watching him race along the sun-bleached dunes toward the beaches, never once turning back, "going after life," as my father liked to call it.

Years later in New York, when I grew to love the sun, I did so like a tourist, never a native. I never knew whether I loved the sun for its own sake, as he did, or because it reminded me of my summer days in Egypt, where I had always avoided sunlight. I liked the sun *from* the shade, the way I like people, not by seeking them out but as though I might any moment lose their friendship and should already learn to live without them. I enter into friendships by scoping out exit doors, sometimes by bolting them shut.

My brother understood people. All I understood were my impressions—which is to say my fictions—of people, as though they and I were alien species and each had learned to pretend the other was not.

When, after Egypt, we began to take long walks together in Rome, he liked to change our itinerary, roam, get lost, explore; I liked to go on the same walks each time, for they led to any one of three to four English-language bookstores or to places that were already familiar or that had reminded me of something I had read in a book and which invariably harked back, when you searched deep and long enough and made all the appropriate transpositions, to something vaguely Alexandrian—as though, for me to feel anything at all, it had to pass through the customhouse not of the senses but of memory. Walking through Rome without groping for inner signposts or without hoping to create new stations to which I might return at some later date would have been totally unthinkable. I wanted him to share my joy each time we repeated a familiar walk or each time it felt as though we were indeed somewhere more familiar than Rome. Understandably, in the end, my brother made fun of my nostalgic antics and, having tired of me, preferred to go out with friends instead.

And yet, though I learned to love my walks without him, I still owe him so many places I wouldn't have discovered had it not been for him—just as, when I went back to Egypt in 1995, I needed to have him present with me all the time, to officiate my return alongside me, else I'd be numb to the experience. Petrarch's walk up Mount Ventoux would mean nothing unless his brother were with him part of the way; Freud's visit to the Acropolis would not cast the dark spell it did without his brother tagging along to remind him of their father; Van Gogh's steadfast Theo was always there to come to his brother's rescue; Wordsworth needed his sister to accompany him on his return to Tintern Abbey. I needed my brother the same way.

When I told him in New York one day that I missed our summer house, he reminded me that as a child I was always the very last to head out to the beach because, as everyone knew, I used to hate the beach, Mediterranean or otherwise.

It was his sense of irony, especially the one he aimed at me for hesitating to eat the falafel sandwich on Passover night in the 1990 version of our late-night walk in Alexandria, that I ended up sacrificing when I decided to kill him off in my memoir in 1995. Of course, he didn't disappear entirely; he came in through a back door when I found myself borrowing my brother's voice in the later version and, with his voice, his love of life and of this earth and of pastries. Suddenly, I loved the sun though I'd always shied away from it. Suddenly, I was the one who loved the odor of stewed meats and the brush of summer heat; I loved people, I loved laughter, and I loved to lie in the sun and doze off with just a fisherman's hat thrown over my face, the smell of the beach forever impressed upon my skin, until that smell became my smell as well, the way Alexandria became my own, though I'd never belonged to it, and never wished to. I had stolen his love because I couldn't feel any of my own.

Was I lying then?

A novel, as the history of the genre from Madame de LaFayette through Defoe, Fielding, Dickens, and Dostoevsky makes abundantly clear, wants to pass for something it is not; it claims to be a history and, as such, narrates events as though they did in fact happen. A memoir, on the other hand, narrates them to read like fiction, which is to say, as though they may never have happened at all. Each borrows the conventions of the other. One tells things as though they were facts, the other as though they were not. A bad memoir may turn out to have a beginning, a middle, and an end. A good novel, like life, sometimes does not.

The distinction between the two is far, far more disquieting than might appear. If writing a memoir is a way of purging the mind of mnemonic deadweight, can lying about these memories or inventing surrogate memories help at all? Does lying actually facilitate such a release, or does it, as should make sense, stand in its way? Or does writing open up a parallel universe into which, one by one, we try to move all of our cherished belongings, the way immigrants, having settled in America, invite, one by one, each of their siblings?

Or is lying about one's life precisely what memoirs are all about, a way of giving one's life a shape and a logic, a coherence it wouldn't have except on paper, a way of returning or of rehearsing such a return, the way some of us would like nothing better than to seek out an old flame, provided the reunion remain a fantasy? Is our life incomplete, incoherent, unless it is given an aesthetic finish? Does a literary sensibility foster the very homesickness that a memoir hopes to redeem? Or does being literary entail the possibility of lying so that, once our lies are embedded in the chronicle of our life, there is no way to remove them, the way it is impossible to remove alloy once a coin is minted or a piece of chewing gum once you've ground it into the pavement?

Friends and readers familiar with the 1990 version of our last seder were stunned to find me taking this farewell night walk by myself in the 1995 version. What had happened to my brother, and why was he not with me on that walk? And, come to think of it, why was he entirely absent from the book? What kind of a *memoir* was this if you can remove one character, tamper with others, and—who knows—invent many others?

Removing my brother from the evening walk turned out to be embarrassingly easy—almost as though getting rid of him had been a lifelong fantasy. Some last-minute alterations had to be made to accommodate the late-night dialogue with my brother to a silent monologue without him. These changes turned out to be unforeseeably propitious, as happens so frequently when we lose a few pages and are forced to rewrite them from scratch only to find that we've managed to say things we would never have thought of saying, and may have been longing to say but couldn't, precisely because the things we had the good fortune to lose had stood in the way. The long elegiac sentences at the very end of *Out of Egypt*, which reviewers quote, were, in fact, written with one purpose only: to smooth out the ridges left by my brother's disappearance, to elegize him away.

> And suddenly I knew, as I touched the damp, grainy surface of the seawall, that I would always remember this night, that in years to come I would remember sitting here, swept with confused longing as I listened to the water lapping the giant boulders beneath the promenade and watched the children head toward the shore in a winding, lambent procession. I wanted to come back tomorrow night, and the night after, and the one after that as well, sensing that what made leaving so fiercely painful was the knowledge that there would never be another night like this, that I would never buy soggy cakes along the coast road in the evening, not this year or any other year, nor feel the baffling, sudden beauty of that moment when, if only for an instant, I had caught myself longing for a city I never knew I loved.

This is not me speaking. It is my brother.

The last sentence, in its original form in *Out of Egypt*, voiced an altogether different sentiment. I had never loved Egypt. Nor had I loved Alexandria, not its odors, not its beaches or its people. In fact, as originally written, this sentence ended with the rather anti-climactic but far more paradoxical words: "I suddenly caught myself longing for a city I never knew I hated." But, by another irony, this statement was not in keeping with the sunny and ebullient portrayal of Alexandria I had adopted throughout the book. My brother loved Alexandria; I hated it.

One of my very first readers immediately sensed this disparity between the word "hate" and the city I seemed to love so much and asked me to . . . reconsider. In light of my affectionate, at times rapturous descriptions of Alexandrian life, wouldn't, perhaps, the word "love" have made more sense?

No one could have been more right. Without a second's doubt, I crossed out the verb "hate" and in its place put down the verb "love." From hating Alexandria, I now loved it. Easy.

That I was able to settle the matter so blithely, almost by flipping a coin, and go from one extreme to the other means either that I nursed ambivalent feelings for the city or that I could not decide who exactly the speaker was at that very instant: my brother or I. But even if it were my brother's voice speaking through mine, my writing about Alexandria in such fond, sensual precision, and with such a yearning to recapture this or that moment, or to revisit this or that site, may have been an undisclosed desire on my part to be like him, to feel as he did, to stop being the person I was, and, if I could convince others that I had, to come to believe it myself.

But there is another confession in store. The night walk on Rue Delta on our last night in Egypt, with or without my brother, never did occur. Everyone stayed home that night, morose and worried as ever, saying farewell to the occasional guests who came by and who, despite our repeated pleas, showed up again on the following morning.

My last walk with my brother in Egypt was simply a fiction. As for the moment when, with or without him, I look out to the sea and promise to remember this very evening on its anniversary in the years to come, it too was a fiction. But this fiction grounded me in a way the truth could never have done. This, to use Aristotle's word, is how I *should* have felt had I taken a last, momentous walk that night.

Indeed, one of the very, very first things I did when I returned to Egypt thirty years later was to head out to Rue Delta to revisit my grandmother's home. On Rue Delta, it kept coming back to me that I hadn't forgotten the slightest thing, which was disappointing but equally comforting. After so many years, I was unable to get lost. I had forgotten nothing. Nothing surprised me. Even the fact that nothing surprised me failed to surprise me. Indeed, I could have stayed home in New York and written about this visit the way I'd written my memoir: at my desk, in front of my computer screen on the Upper West Side. All I kept thinking on returning to Alexandria was that I've read Proust, I've studied, taught and written about memory, written from memory, I know all the ins and outs of time and of prememory, postmemory, paramemory, of place visited, unvisited, revisited, and yet, as I look at these familiar buildings, this street, these people, and realize I am failing to feel anything but numbness, all I can think of is they're already in my book. Writing about them had made them so familiar, that it was as if I'd never been away. Writing about Alexandria, the capital of memory, had robbed memory of its luster.

On Rue Delta, the way to the sea seemed already paved for me. I began walking down a street that had not changed in thirty years. Even its odors, rising as they once did from street level to my bedroom three flights up, were not strange enough, while the odor of falafel brought to mind a falafel hole-in-the-wall on Broadway and 104th that had frequently made me think of the tiny summertime establishments in Alexandria, whose falafel now, ironically, smelled less authentic in Egypt than the falafel on Broadway.

I had only to look at the way Rue Delta led to the shore and I instantly remembered writing the scene about my brother and how he and I had walked there on our last night in Egypt. All I remembered was not what had happened here decades ago but simply the fiction I'd written. I remembered something I knew was a lie. We had stopped here, purchased something to eat, and then crossed the coast road and heaved ourselves up to sit on that exact same spot on a stone wall along the seafront, watching the Mediterranean by night with its constellation of fishing boats glimmering on the horizon. I could see my brother as he was then and as he is now, gazing at the wild procession of Egyptian children waving their Ramadan lanterns along the sand banks, disappearing behind a jetty, reappearing farther off along the shore. I tried to remind myself that he was no longer present in the final version of this very scene, that I'd removed him from it and that I'd sat overlooking the sea by myself. But however I tried to reason with the memory of that first version, he kept popping back on Rue Delta, as though his image, like a Freudian screen memory, or like an afterimage, a shadow memory, no matter how many times I suppressed it, were a truth that it was pointless, even dishonest, to dismiss, even though I knew I had never been on that walk with or without him.

Today, when I try to visualize Rue Delta by night, the only picture that comes to mind is the one with my brother. He is wearing shorts, a sweater slung around his neck, and is headed to the seafront, already savoring the sandwich he is planning to buy at a corner shop called the Falafel Pasha. I have no other memories of Rue Delta. Even the memory of my return visit has begun to fade. What I certainly can't remember is the real Rue Delta, the Rue Delta as I envisioned it before writing *Out of Egypt*. That Rue Delta is forever lost.

D. J. WALDIE

Public Policy / Private Lives

· · ·

WITH AN EXCERPT FROM
Holy Land: A Suburban Memoir

FROM *Holy Land: A Suburban Memoir*

In 1949, three developers bought 3,500 acres of Southern California farm-land. They planned to build something that was not exactly a city.

In 1950, before the work of roughing the foundations and pouring concrete began, the three men hired a young photographer with a single-engine plane to document their achievement from the air.

The photographer flew when the foundations of the first houses were poured. He flew again, when the framing was done and later, when the roofers were nearly finished. He flew over the shell of the shopping center that explains this and many other California suburbs.

The three developers were pleased with the results. The black-and-white photographs show immense abstractions on ground the color of the full moon.

Some of the photographs appeared in *Fortune* and other magazines. The developers bound enlargements in a handsome presentation book. I have several pages from one of the copies.

The photographs celebrate house frames precise as cells in a hive and stucco walls fragile as an unearthed bone. Seen from above, the grid is beautiful and terrible.

My father's kindness was as pure and indifferent as a certain kind of saint's.

My father did not have a passion for his giving; it came from him, perhaps after much spiritual calculation, as a product might come from a conveyer belt.

The houses in this suburb were built the same way. As many as a hundred a day were begun between 1950 and 1952, more than five hundred a week. No two floor plans were built next to each other; no neighbor had to stare into his reflection across the street.

Teams of men built the houses.

Some men poured concrete into the ranks of foundations from mixing trucks waiting in a mile-long line. Other men threw down floors nailed with pneumatic hammers, tilted up the framing, and scaled the rafters with cedar shingles lifted by conveyer belts from the beds of specially built trucks.

You are mistaken if you consider this a criticism, either of my father or the houses.

◆ ◆ ◆

Public Policy / Private Lives

I am a memoirist—a somewhat disreputable calling, given the elastic way in which some memoirists have recently treated the facts in their stories. Admissions of fictionalizing rightly cause general suspicion of the kind of writing for which I'm best known.* Worse, I am a memoirist of the everyday—a suburban memoirist!—and I half wish that I could substitute dysfunctions in place of the commonplace way the light falls through the parkway trees of Lakewood, my nondescript Southern California neighborhood, or the flatness of its landscape, or the smallness of its mass-produced houses.

Could anyone—why would anyone—make up so much ordinariness? What use would it have?

Los Angeles is often cast as an extraordinary place—so lacking the ordinary that it almost ceases to exist. At the end of the movie *Chinatown,* at the end of all the false leads about water and power that clueless private eye Jake Gittes has doggedly run down, when Jake's partner pulls him back from the sight of Evelyn Mulwray's bullet-shattered face and the Chinese faces of the gawking bystanders crowd into the frame, and the meaning of Los Angeles is summed up with the line: *Forget it, Jake. It's Chinatown . . .* in the end, Los Angeles is Chinatown, and nothing beyond Chinatown. The story of the city

---

* This essay expands on a presentation made at Loyola Marymount University of Los Angeles in February 2006, a few days after James Frey acknowledged the fictionalizing in his best-selling memoir *A Million Little Pieces,* which included fabricated details about his criminal record, drug use, and drug rehabilitation experiences.

has dwindled to a conclusion we are powerless to affect, like a land-scape watched in the rearview mirror of a car fleeing a crime scene. Robert Towne's fable of murder, greed, incest, and hydraulics insists that all of us in Los Angeles are only along for the ride in a city full of ugly enigmas.

Seen from the shadows of a black-and-white film or imprisoned in the glare of its celebrity culture, Los Angeles looks like a collection of absences: the absence of serious architecture, of urban intensity, of a center, of authenticity, and often, just the absence of New York. Finally, we are absent from the city, too, wrapped in our own reveries of another Los Angeles that is more adequate to the demands of desire. As the cultural critic Norman Klein has made clear, projecting our own absence onto the blank and indifferent landscape of the city necessarily makes Los Angeles a place of substitution and forgetting. Klein calls this problem "erasure," and he locates it within a larger critique of modernism in its relation to the subordination, displacement, and substitution of memories.

You and I can recite this city's defeated, substituted recollections about itself like a catechism lesson: an elderly John Huston stole the water of the Owens Valley in 1934 (just as *Chinatown* proved, although that isn't the way it happened). And a cartoon Dr. Doom shut down the beloved trolley lines to make way for freeways (just as *Who Framed Roger Rabbit?* showed, although that isn't exactly true, either). Because we've seen *True Confessions* and *L.A. Confidential, Lost Highway* and *Blade Runner*, we have a sick certainty that we know what kind of dystopia Los Angeles is.

The sunny narratives of Los Angelenos were made for the freeway's fluidity, but that's mostly gone now in gridlock and gas prices, and now our stories are trapped in brown neighborhoods on the city's working-class flatlands, or broken down on cul-de-sac streets among mini-malls that all look alike with signs written in characters that are meaningful only to the neighborhood. But for the gridlock, a lot of us would be just passing through Los Angeles—where some are perpetual tourists and never citizens—on our way to newer and brighter suburbs in Montana or Las Vegas or to some internal exile of the spirit within the gates of a guarded subdivision or behind a security sign that promises "immediate armed response."

Because of this city's Catholic past, its capture in the Mexican War and later fears of Mexican irredentism, its primal dread of race mixing, its speculative cycles of economic boom and bust, and the seductive power of its extravagant sales pitch, Los Angeles is perpetually shadowed by its noir double: the city of unmet desires, the city of willful amnesia, the disillusioned city that naïvely buys its own illusions, the city embodied in Phyllis Dietrichson's house in *Double Indemnity*: sunny and phony on the outside and shuttered and menacing on the inside—a place for plotting murder.

We hunger for stories in Los Angeles. In a city of amnesiacs, there are only a few narrative arcs that shadow our daily lives:

• The story of Los Angeles is an elegy for a place of former perfection . . . a perfect place, once upon a time . . . and that time was just before your new next-door neighbor arrived. That's our history of regret.

• Or the story of Los Angeles is merely a perversion, in which every booster cliché conceals a menace: the city's balmy climate is actually lousy (tornadoes today and drought tomorrow) and the indulgent landscape is really lethal (when it isn't burning with wildfires or shaking with earthquakes, it's crawling with mountain lions with a taste for suburban white meat). In its contempt for its subject—in its conviction that we're just along for the ride—that storyline is our pornography.

• Or the story of Los Angeles is just a spectacle. "The splendors and miseries of Los Angeles," Reyner Banham says, "the graces and grotesqueries, appear to me as unrepeatable as they are unprecedented."* If Los Angeles is the great exception—a city without a heritage or

---

* *Los Angeles: The Architecture of Four Ecologies* (1971; Berkeley and Los Angeles: University of California Press, 2001), 6.

legacy—then its story may be glamorous, but it's just another lurid burlesque, best witnessed while slightly intoxicated.

• Or the story of Los Angeles is a blank, or as Pico Iyer says, a "space waiting to be claimed by whatever dream or destiny you wanted to throw at it."* That's our daydream of the city of the future, a restless landscape twitching with big ideas about building the next utopia on the demolished premises of the last one. What's broken in each convulsion isn't just ground; it's the thread of memory. And it's these broken threads that make too many of us homeless here, even if we have a house.

Because none of these frameworks—regret, contempt, burlesque, or irony—satisfies for very long, many of its residents believe that Los Angeles is an unnecessary city. And that belief—abetted by memory substitution and deliberate forgetting—has been the precondition for the past forty years of failed public policy in Los Angeles toward immigrants, commuters, ethnic communities, small-business operators, the homeless and working poor, homeowners, and taxpayers.

Those of us who expose our lives in public in memoirs will appeal to sentiment as our reason to write, or emotional truth or justice or generational continuity or historical redress or personal therapy or tribal solidarity or just Whitman's "barbaric yawp over the roofs of the world." But some of us take the memoir—as I do—as a form of political speech.

Memory, after all, is the material basis of public policy. Memory insistently reminds us that contingencies dominate the experience of our lives, that time's arrow will not be stayed by nostalgia, and that authority seeks always to substitute its official recollections for those we have labored so hard to hold. Remembering is an act of courage in Los Angeles, even if we do not fully understand the stories we have

* Quoted in the documentary *Los Angeles Now,* produced and directed by Phillip Rodriguez (2004).

to tell. Memory is sabotage against the city's regime of speed. I have the impression that the disturbing qualities of life here that most commentators remark on—and the tendency of Los Angeles to self-immolate in civil discord—reflect a tragic failure to remember. Yet despite all of our efforts to forget them or find replacements for them, the stories of Los Angeles will bleed through the clichés as if the stories themselves knew how much we need them. The persistent "hunger of memory," in the words of Richard Rodriguez, is as familiar and feral in Los Angeles as the coyote standing watchfully in the middle of the street in my suburban neighborhood before it trots into the tall grass under the Edison Company power lines.

I live in a place of presumed exile—in a tract house on a block of more tract houses in Lakewood, a neighborhood hardly distinguishable from the next and all of them extending as far as the street grid allows in a metropolis with thousands of miles of streets all just the same. The hunger of memory is acute here, but it is only a localization of the larger experience of California, which itself is only a portion of the immigrant experience of the West; and the problem of the West is only an especially perplexing subset of the everlasting problem of America, which is *how to make a home here.*

We long for a home but doubt its worth when we have it. We depend on a place but dislike its claims on us. Each of us is certain about our own preferences for a home, but we're ready to question *your* choice. And no place is immune from the peculiarly American certainty that something better—something more adequate to the demands of our desire—is just beyond the next bend in the road.

Los Angeles, as a representation of the divided American heart, poses large questions about the uses of memory, and this bears on the memoirist's hope: *Can any part of our past be of any value to us except as nostalgia or irony? Do the places where we grew up have legitimate claims on us?* We find it difficult to talk coherently about issues of place in Los Angeles, which inevitably leads to confusion in public policies about the best means to make our home there. Which is not homeowner determinism—locally expressed in Southern California as a fierce NIMBY-ism.

Lacking a usable rhetoric of place, burdened by a history of regret, and unencumbered by our stories, the makers of public policy in Los Angeles have failed to give the region what it critically needs—and that is not more planning, not more government, and not even the delivery of more housing and jobs. What is needed is more place-bound loyalty.

Wes Jackson of the Land Institute insisted that Americans had not yet become native to their land. His subject was rural America; mine is the suburb, but the question is true for both places and true on the same terms as well. Every American place is a ruined paradise that demands a common effort to repair—a ruined paradise, and therefore someone's home. We can no longer afford to erase our homes out of forgetfulness—or worse, out of willful amnesia—and instead imagine, as many want to in Los Angeles, that they live in a historyless city, a placelessness devoid of us and our sacred ordinariness. We cannot afford to be merely sojourners in Los Angeles.

One source of the narrative tradition about the making and unmaking of places to live begins with the story of the ruin of a city. There are men and gods in the *Iliad*, and we like to think the story is about them. But the story is really about the fate of places. All cities are like Troy in their potential to mingle tragedy and the everyday. Every city ultimately disappoints, Homer knew, and therefore is to be cherished while you can. Imaginatively, westerners live in sacred Ilium, in a town where the cost of an ordinary life is loyalty to an imperfect place. It is good to recall that every city claims someone's allegiance, answers someone's longing, and persists in someone's memory. And one task of the memoirist is, like Homer, to bring us to these awful realizations.

My particular place is at the extreme southeast corner of Los Angeles County in a 957-square-foot house of wood frame and stucco construction put up hastily during World War II on dead-level farm-

land just far enough from a Douglas Aircraft plant that bombs dropped
by Japanese planes might miss it. I live in a neighborhood on the
edge of the great flat of the Los Angeles plain between the Los Angeles
and San Gabriel rivers not far from oil refineries, and I actually
imagine that the place in which I live is, in Josiah Royce's terms, a
"beloved community."* I acquired my sense of place here and later
my belief that a sense of place, like a sense of self, is part of the equipment of a conscious mind.

My parents bought my house in 1946, less than a year after the
war ended, and they felt extraordinarily lucky. My older brother was
born into this house in October that year, and I followed in 1948. My
mother died from this house in 1979. My father died in it in 1982.
I've lived nowhere else. The idea of a mass-produced suburb was still
new when my brother and I were boys, and no one knew then what
would happen when tens of thousands of working-class husbands
and wives—so young and inexperienced—were thrown together
and expected to make a fit place to live.

Maybe you wouldn't regard a house like mine as a place of pil-
grimage, but my parents did. Perhaps their one big move, from the
Depression in New York and through the world war to here, on the
edge of Los Angeles, had been enough. My parents were grateful for
the comforts of their not-quite-middle-class life. Their aspirations
weren't for *more* but only for *enough*. Their lives together seemed to
be about that, too—about the idea of enough. Their neighbors had
the same idea (despite the claims of critics then and now, who assume all suburban places are about excess). Despite everything that
was ignored or squandered in making my suburb, I believe a kind of
dignity was gained. More men than just my father have said to me

* American philosopher Josiah Royce coined the phrase "beloved community"
in *The Problem of Christianity* (New York: Macmillan, 1913). He wrote, "Since
the office of religion is to aim towards the creation on earth of the Beloved
Community, the future task of religion is the task of inventing and applying the
arts which shall win men over to unity, and which shall overcome their original hatefulness by the gracious love, not of mere individuals, but of communities" (p. 430).

that living here gave them a life made whole and habits that did not make them feel ashamed.

My neighborhood was one of the places where suburban stories were first mass-produced. They were stories then for displaced Okies and Arkies, Jews who knew the pain of exclusion, Catholics, too, and anyone white with a steady job. Today, the same stories begin here, except the anxious people who tell them are as completely mixed in their colors and ethnicities as they can be. I continue to live here because I want to find out what happens next to these new narrators of stories I think I already know.

I once thought my suburban life was an extended lesson in how to get along with other people. Now, I think the lesson isn't neighborliness; it's humility. Perhaps that's because I am one of those Catholics, too, who lives in a California suburb built all at once in 1950—17,500 houses in thirty-three months!—and when I stand at the end of my block, I see a pattern of sidewalk, driveway, and lawn that aspires to be no more than harmless. I somehow see that as a sign of faithfulness, or at least of loyalty. We live in a time now of great harm to the ordinary parts of our lives, and I wish that I had acquired all the faithfulness my neighborhood offers.

What kind of imagination is at work to prompt that absurd claim? It's not idiosyncratic or exclusive to me. The imagination at work is particular and peculiar in ways that I'll call "Catholic."*

"Catholics live in an enchanted world," Andrew Greeley asserts in the opening pages of his extended essay on the Catholic imagination.† "A world," he says, "of statues and holy water, stained glass and votive candles, saints and religious medals, rosary beads and holy pictures. But these Catholic paraphernalia are merely hints of a deeper and more pervasive religious sensibility that inclines Catholics to see

* Or, to put it another way, I am seeking an epistemology of everyday life that can include Los Angeles as an instance.
† Andrew M. Greeley, *The Catholic Imagination* (Berkeley and Los Angeles: University of California Press, 2000).

the Holy lurking in creation. The world of the Catholic is haunted by a sense that the objects, events, and persons of daily life are revelations of Grace."

Some of those revelations are habits, which Flannery O'Connor might have called "habits of being." Greeley has said that Catholics remain Catholic because they like to be Catholic, which he ties to the imaginative life that even humdrum, everyday Catholicism makes habitual. But some revelations of grace are things themselves, and that, I suppose, is my own bias. We touch the much-handled things we grew up with, and they touch us back, a relationship that implies a sacramental extension, a corresponding touch that you might rightly mistake for God's. All of my writing is, in part, a meditation on the fate of ordinary things—the things we touch and the lingering effects of their touch on us. Manipulation is precisely what happens, but it works both ways. What we seek, I think, is tenderness in the encounter, but that goes both ways, too. In some of us, however, the touch of the everyday inspires dread. The imagination dwells on what Joan Didion memorably called "the unspeakable peril of the everyday."

And some revelations of grace, as O'Connor might have said, are encounters that render you so wounded by grief or exaltation that divinity infects you; encounters that gut your self-regard. As Stephen Schloesser has noted, in locating the roots of the twentieth-century Catholic novel, some Catholic writers sought to "out-grotesque the grotesque" in order to show that behind even the ugliest phenomena—even suburban sprawl, in my case—there is a supernatural force at work. "God lurks everywhere," Greeley told an interviewer from *Religion & Ethics Newsweekly* in 2002. "That's the fundamental Catholic instinct: That on the imaginative and poetic level, God is lurking everywhere. Right down the street, right around the corner, there's God."

This imaginative apprehension of the immanent in the everyday has a *political* outcome—that is, the establishment of a sympathetic bond between strangers who might be neighbors leading to shared acts of community building. As much as it is a sense of wonder and delight, the Catholic imagination, as Greeley sees it, is a tool that helps men and women trust one another and to be faithful to each other, and that faithfulness supports our efforts to form communities and to breed in them O'Connor's habits of being.

One habit of being that I regard as a grace is a sense of place. When I walk out the door of my home, I see the familiar pattern of house, street, parks, places of worship, schools, and stores. I see the human-scale, porous, and specific landscape into which was poured the ordinariness that has shaped my work, my convictions, and my aspirations. My sense of place is based on the belief that each of us has an imaginative, inner landscape compounded of memory and longing that seeks to be connected to an outer landscape of people and circumstances.

The author and environmentalist Barry Lopez asked a question some years ago about the San Fernando Valley,* like Lakewood another place of terrible ordinariness. For Lopez a sense of place doesn't begin with any of the conventional markers of community building: institutions, political processes, or assertions of a tradition. He asked a more insightful question: "How can we become vulnerable to a place?" With the deepening and widening of our imagination as an aspect of faith, we become more and more trusting. In becoming vulnerable, we acquire a sense of place. With that sensibility, we become implicated in a particular history and the common stories that bear our individual and shared memories.

Trust, vulnerability, and a capacity for stories: it is with these habits that we become loyal. It's really a question of falling in love. "In an enchanted world," Greeley writes, "the beloved is both enchanted and frustrating." We cannot, or will not, understand the reason why attraction to a place and its circumstances asks so much of us, but we act on that desire, which lets us yearn for what we already have.

* Barry Lopez, "A Scary Abundance of Water," *Los Angeles Weekly,* January 9, 2002.

There's an education in straight and narrow streets when they are bordered by sidewalks and a shallow setback of twenty feet of lawn and framed by unassuming houses set close enough together that the density is about eight units per acre. With neighbors just fifteen feet apart, we're easily in each other's lives in my suburb—across fences, in front yards, and even through the thin stucco-over-chicken-wire of house walls. You don't have to love all of the possibilities for civility handed to us roughly by these circumstances, but you have to love enough of them.

The strength of that regard, Royce thought, might be enough to form an intentional community—a community of memory—even if the place is as synthetic as a mass-produced suburb or the sudden gold rush towns of California that Royce was recalling in the 1870s. I believe Royce was right: at a minimum, loyalty to the idea of loyalty is necessary, even if the object of our loyalty is uncertain. There are no perfect places, only places where memories and longings may persist. Paul Wilkes, in his review of Greeley's *The Catholic Imagination*, referred to this sensibility as "sympathetic pragmatism."*

And then for some of us, that feeling evaporates into disregard. After all, we're well-trained consumers, TV remote control in hand, and ready to switch channels or affections or hometowns whenever we're distracted. We run the risk, of course, of becoming so distracted that the imaginative connections between inner and outer landscapes break down entirely.

I don't really know how to make myself more vulnerable to the place in which I find myself (or perhaps I do, but only dimly). But faithfulness to what can be found in its history—to what can be found in our shared stories—impels me forward, drawn into a problematic landscape by the pragmatic sympathies of a Catholic imagination.

The imagination is a power of appropriation that, like the Word being made flesh, enmeshes the ghostly and the definite. That entanglement is experienced, for writers like me (I suppose) as a dialogue, a

* Paul Wilkes, "A Sense of Sacred," *America*, April 8, 2000.

continuous narrative within and without that I understand to be prayer. Because my imagination inclines to being analogical, habitual, communitarian, and commonplace, I assume that it's Catholic. The complication for that imagination, as Mark Ravizza has noted,* is the appeal of the too domesticated, a tendency he notes in Greeley's conception of an analogical imagination framed by statues, stained-glass windows, gilded altarpieces, tapestries, votive candles, rosary beads, and holy cards.

There's more, of course, than all this lovely kitsch. My faith uses ordinary things from the marketplace: oil, bread, salt, wine, and wax. It values unappealing debris that everyday life leaves behind: bones, mummified remains, and, in the form of analogs, blood and broken flesh. After all, the Catholic imagination must consider daily the consequences of a state-sanctioned murder by public torture. For pilgrims journeying through the Cathedral of Our Lady of the Angels in Los Angeles, a contemporary manifestation of the Catholic imagination as an entire landscape, the end of the journey is Simon Toparovsky's life-sized bronze figure of a man, black skin flayed, nailed up to a post. There is nothing sentimental in that image, no appeal to a consoling immigrant Catholic experience of folk piety. It isn't possible to be nostalgic about a crucifixion.

In his defense of the analogical (or sacramental) imagination as an accomplice of faith, Greeley offers a beloved aesthetics. "I am still a Catholic," he writes in *Why I Am a Catholic*, "because of the beauty of Catholicism, beauty being truth in its most attractive form. It is the beauty of the images and stories of Catholicism which keep me in the Church."†

But sometimes the analogies are weak; beautiful effects fail to materialize. During the sermon at one Sunday mass at the Los Angeles cathedral, the altar servers brought out a large brazier to help illus-

---

* Mark Ravizza, "Polluted Protagonists and the Enduring Appeal of the Catholic Imagination," *Explore* (Spring 2002).
† Kevin and Marilyn Ryan, eds., *Why I Am a Catholic* (New York: Riverhead Books, 1998).

trate a point the celebrant was making about the nature of prayer. He poured a handful of incense onto the coals and more incense until flames drove up a thick column of gray smoke. I anticipated that the cloying odor of liturgical incense—a powerful instigator of Catholic memories—would fill the air. It didn't. By an accident of geometry in the design of the nave or its superior ventilation, the cloud ascended, spread into a veil, and joined the indifferent light overhead. But the burning incense left no smell.

In the Catholic imagination, the Holy haunts the everyday, but so does disappointment. As Greeley notes, because the Catholic imagination believes that everything is a sign, it is prone, in its disappointments, to superstition, cults, and the substitution of religion for faith, the replacement of authority for loyalty. The brokenhearted can make a redemptive turning to the Incarnate, or they can turn away to the idols of institutions and ideologies or their own comforts.

I'm satisfied because my imagination *dwells* (on and in a community), but I'm anxious that having a Catholic imagination will *unsettle* me, too. That imagination should flinch when blows are laid on another's back, lift in sympathy with the prayers of another's worship, and savor another's wisdom even when expressed in cadences that are wholly foreign. It's a sacramental imagination, surely, but also a moral one, and it is the means both by which I have written myself into the story of my place and its mix of tragedies and joys and through which I have negotiated my way from the personal to the public, from a flawed private life to the flawed—but sacred, human, and humanizing—body of the ruined paradise where I have a home.

Because I believe every American place is the habitat of memory, I believe every American place can have an ecology of hope.

In its false representations, Los Angeles is preferentially the shrouded city of "treacherous unbrightness," in Faulkner's bleak phrase: the city that always cheats on its lovers, that is always painted in the colors of smog, the city always seen from a height, from a freeway overpass, from a seat in a descending jetliner, the hapless observer

always going under, down to a carcinogenic sea. That imagined place
continues to frame issues of place in Los Angeles and the public policies intended to resolve them. Today, mythic Los Angeles—that
monstrous and forgetful city—is slowly succumbing to the moral
imaginations of many new interpreters who meld history, personal
essay, and the techniques of the memoir to tell a refigured story of
the city that contains more about us and what we find familiar and
what we yearn for. And it's not *Chinatown*. This is the form of public
speech that the contemplation of my private life has led me to, and
I am not alone in this enterprise, which is nothing less than the
reimagining of Los Angeles, a task all of its residents have been un-
willingly drafted for.

Other memoirists acknowledge that they write to preserve and
commemorate or to indict and condemn or to discover and then reveal the reasons for their scars or to school the troubled in the art of
self-healing or simply to echo the epilogue of Moby Dick, taken from
the Book of Job: *And I only am escaped alone to tell thee.* I am bent
in another direction—toward works of the imagination that can be
picked up (as a tool might be) for immediate use in the labor of making a sustainable city. We all live on land we've wounded by our being
here. Yet we must be here or be nowhere and have nothing with which
to make our lives together. How should one act knowing that making
a home requires this? How should I regard my neighbors, complicit
with me in making our place? It's possible to answer with fury or
neglect. It's possible to be so assured of privilege that contempt for
a place like mine is the only answer. It's possible to be so rootless that
these questions are merely ironic.

The stories we will tell each other in the process of making Los
Angeles more ordinary will inevitably be partial. But the best of those
stories will resist the subordination of the everyday. We can give in
to a malign tradition of forgetfulness or benefit from a shared process
of truth and reconciliation. The stories we will share in the process,
I believe, will redeem us.

Acknowledgments

This collection of essays emerged from a spirited series of public readings and panel discussions we organized, held during the winter and spring of 2007 at the University of Minnesota in Minneapolis. The series was called "Who's Got the Story—Memoir as History/History as Memoir," and it remains available on line at www .whosgotthestory.umn.edu.

We are most grateful to the University of Minnesota community and its many interrelated constituencies that made possible the original series and provided support for the essays here. In particular, we wish to acknowledge major funding from the University's McKnight Arts and Humanities Endowment, the Institute for Advanced Study, and the College of Liberal Arts Scholarly Events Fund. Without their substantial contributions and encouragement, our ambition would have been much diminished.

The generous co-sponsorship of a wide array of departments and programs at the University of Minnesota demonstrates the broadly based interest in questions of narrative truth in history and literature. We are grateful to our colleagues across campus for their support and wish to salute with thanks the departments, programs and units that helped the project: American Studies; English; Creative Writing; History; Frederick R. Weisman Art Museum; Austrian Studies; Cultural Studies and Comparative Literature; Gay, Lesbian, Bisexual, Transgender and Ally Programs Office; Gender, Women, and Sexuality Studies; German and European Studies; Global Studies;

Holocaust and Genocide Studies; Immigration History Research Center; Jewish Studies; Journalism and Mass Communications; the Center for the Study of Politics and Governance; and the Office of University Women.

Ami Berger, as communications manager for the School of Journalism and Mass Communications, provided essential counsel for the original series, and Deb Lawton designed the striking poster. We are grateful as well to Karen A. Bencke, software and web development coordinator at the College of Liberal Arts Office of Information and to Zach Taylor for web design. The series was taped for video archive by Richard Stachow, video photographer in CLA TV Production.

Community support from Paulette Warren and the Loft Literary Center was a great benefit and provided another reminder of the cultural vibrancy of the Twin Cities, as did support from the Minnesota Historical Society.

Special thanks to panel moderators, Professor Madelon Sprengnether (English and Creative Writing) and Regents Professor Sara Evans (History) for their deft management of the public forums, and to Cheri Register for her thoughtful reflections, even though the panel itself was snowed out.

We are grateful to Professor Ann Waltner, director of the University's Institute for Advanced Study, and Susannah Smith, the Institute's managing director, for their generous and inventive collaboration and steadfast encouragement. Jeanne Kilde offered valuable counsel on grant applications. Karen Kinoshita, also from the Institute for Advanced Study, was our angel of organization, working magic with complicated travel and scheduling arrangements. We are grateful as well to Borealis Books and the anthology's editor, Ann Regan, for her energetic involvement in the project and her meticulous response to the essays, and to Will Powers, design and production manager, for bringing the collection together so attractively.

Marly Rusoff of Rusoff and Associates Literary Agency offered sage advice and was unfailingly gracious and encouraging. And on the home front we happily acknowledge the patience and solidarity over long months of our husbands, Terrence Williams and Lary May.

Matt Becker joined us first as an indispensable assistant to the original series and later as a full member of our editorial team. The three of us worked together for over a year on matters small and sweeping. It is impossible to imagine this book without his enormous contribution. We gladly and gratefully acknowledge that our single greatest debt is to him.

Contributors

ANDRÉ ACIMAN is the author of *Out of Egypt: A Memoir* (1994); *False Papers: Essays on Exile and Memory* (2000); and the novel *Call Me by Your Name* (2007). He has also coauthored and edited *The Proust Project* (2004) and *Letters of Transit* (1999). Born in Alexandria, he lived in Italy and France. He received his Ph.D. from Harvard University and has taught at Princeton University and Bard College; he is currently the chair of the CUNY Graduate Center's Doctoral Program in Comparative Literature and the director of its Writers' Institute. He has received a Whiting Writers' Award, a Guggenheim Fellowship, and a fellowship from the New York Public Library's Cullman Center for Scholars and Writers. His work has appeared in the *New York Times, New Yorker, New York Review of Books, New Republic*, and *Paris Review*, as well as in several volumes of *The Best American Essays*.

MATT BECKER is an assistant editor and the rights and permissions manager at Wayne State University Press. He has taught at the University of Minnesota, where he earned his Ph.D. in American studies. His dissertation, "The Edge of Darkness: Youth Culture Since the 1960s," explores the relationship between civic disengagement among young people and their embrace of gothic popular culture over the past forty-five years. He has published in *The Velvet Light Trap* and elsewhere. He helped organize the conference series on memoir and history from which this collection of essays developed.

JUNE CROSS is an associate professor at Columbia University's Graduate School of Journalism. She brings thirty years of experience—

earned as reporter, correspondent, and producer in positions at PBS and CBS—to the craft of documentary filmmaking. *Secret Daughter,* her autobiographical documentary, aired on *Frontline* in 1996 and won both a duPont-Columbia Journalism Award for Excellence in Broadcast Journalism and an Emmy for Outstanding Cultural Programming; she later published a memoir by the same title. She was an executive producer for *This Far by Faith,* a six-part PBS series on the African American religious experience, and her most recent documentary follows the struggle of a New Orleans family over two years as they rebuild their lives.

CARLOS EIRE was one of fourteen thousand unaccompanied Cuban children airlifted to the United States in the early 1960s. After living for three and a half years in a succession of foster homes, he and his brother were finally reunited with their mother in Chicago in 1965. His father was never allowed to leave Cuba. He taught at St. John's University in Minnesota and the University of Virginia and was a member of the Institute for Advanced Study in Princeton before joining the faculty of Yale University in 1996, where he is now the T. Lawrason Riggs Professor of History and Religious Studies. He has published several books on late medieval and early modern Europe; his memoir of the Cuban Revolution, *Waiting for Snow in Havana: Confessions of a Cuban Boy* (2003), won the National Book Award for nonfiction in 2003 and has been translated into several languages.

HELEN EPSTEIN is the author of five books of literary nonfiction, including *Children of the Holocaust* (1979) and *Where She Came From: A Daughter's Search for Her Mother's History* (1997), a memoir and social history of two hundred years of Central European Jewish life. Those, and her biography *Joe Papp: An American Life* (1994), were named New York Times Notable Books of the Year. She was the first tenured woman professor in New York University's journalism department and for two decades freelanced for the Sunday *New York*

Times and other national publications, writing profiles of cultural figures such as art historian Meyer Schapiro and musicians Vladimir Horowitz, Leonard Bernstein, and Yo Yo Ma. A full list of her publications is available at www.helenepstein.com.

SAMUEL G. FREEDMAN is the author of *Small Victories: The Real World of a Teacher, Her Students and Their High School* (1990; National Book Award finalist, 1990); *Upon This Rock: The Miracles of a Black Church* (1993; Helen Bernstein Award for Excellence in Journalism, 1993); *The Inheritance: How Three Families and America Moved from Roosevelt to Reagan and Beyond* (1996; Pulitzer Prize finalist, 1997); *Jew vs. Jew: The Struggle for the Soul of American Jewry* (2000; National Jewish Book Award for Non-Fiction, 2001); *Who She Was: A Son's Search for His Mother's Life* (2005); and *Letters to a Young Journalist* (2006). Formerly a staff reporter for the *New York Times*, Freedman writes the paper's "On Education" column. He has contributed to numerous other publications, including the *Jerusalem Post*, *USA Today*, *New York*, *Rolling Stone*, *Salon*, and BeliefNet. A tenured professor at the Columbia University Graduate School of Journalism, Freedman was named the nation's outstanding journalism educator in 1997 by the Society of Professional Journalists.

PATRICIA HAMPL's books include the memoirs *A Romantic Education* (1981) and *Virgin Time* (1992), two poetry collections, and *Spillville* (1987), a prose meditation on Antonin Dvořák in Iowa. *I Could Tell You Stories* (1999), her book of essays about memory, was a finalist for the National Book Critics Circle Award (2000). Her recent books, *Blue Arabesque* (2006) and *The Florist's Daughter* (2007), were both New York Times Notable Books of the Year. She has received fellowships from the Guggenheim and Bush Foundations and National Endowment for the Arts. She was a 1995 Fulbright Fellow to the Czech Republic. In 1990 she was awarded a MacArthur Fellowship. She is Regents Professor at the University of Minnesota and serves on the permanent faculty of the Prague Summer Program.

FENTON JOHNSON was born ninth of nine children into a Kentucky whiskey-making family with a strong storytelling tradition. He is the author of two novels, *Crossing the River* (1989) and *Scissors, Paper, Rock* (1993), as well as *Geography of the Heart: A Memoir* (1996; Lambda Literary Award, 1996, and American Library Association Stonewall Book Award, 1997) and *Keeping Faith: A Skeptic's Journey among Christian and Buddhist Monks* (2003; Kentucky Literary Award and Lambda Literary Award, 2004). Johnson has written for *Harper's Magazine*, the *New York Times Magazine*, and many literary quarterlies, and he contributes occasional commentaries to National Public Radio. He has received numerous literary awards, among them a Guggenheim Fellowship, a James Michener Fellowship from the Iowa Writers Workshop, and National Endowment for the Arts Fellowships in both fiction and creative nonfiction. He serves on the faculty of the creative writing program at the University of Arizona. Additional information is available at www.fentonjohnson.com.

ALICE KAPLAN is the Lehrman Professor of Romance Studies and a professor of literature and history at Duke University. A native Minnesotan, she received her Ph.D. in French from Yale University in 1981. She is the author of several books on twentieth-century French literature and cultural history, including *Reproductions of Banality: Fascism, Literature, and French Intellectual Life* (1986) and *French Lessons* (1993), an autobiographical account of her passion for the French language. *The Collaborator* (2000) was named a Notable Book of the Year by the *New York Times* and American Library Association and won the Los Angeles Times Book Award in history in 2000. *The Interpreter* (2005) was awarded the 2006 Henry Adams Prize by the Society for History in the Federal Government. Kaplan is also a literary translator, most notably of Roger Grenier. Her latest translation is Evelyne Bloch-Dano's *Madame Proust* (2007), a biography of Proust's mother.

ANNETTE KOBAK, born in London of a Czechoslovak father and English mother, studied modern languages at Cambridge University and creative writing at the University of East Anglia. Her first book, *Isabelle* (1988), about the short, dramatic life of nineteenth-century traveler Isabelle Eberhardt, was published in several languages and made into a BBC2 film in the series *Great Journeys*. She also translated Isabelle's only novel, *Vagabond*, from the French. Her book *Joe's War: My Father Decoded* (2004), described as a "super-eclectic mix of travelogue, oral testimony, autobiography and historical documents" and widely reviewed in America and the United Kingdom, was chosen as Book of the Week on BBC Radio 4. She has reviewed fiction, biography, memoir, and travel writing for the *New York Times Book Review* and the *Times Literary Supplement,* and she presented the series *The Art of Travel* on BBC Radio 4. Annette lives in London, where she is currently Royal Literary Fund Writing Fellow at Kingston University.

MICHAEL PATRICK MACDONALD is the author of *All Souls: A Family Story from Southie* (1999) and of *Easter Rising: A Memoir of Roots and Rebellion* (2006). He has won an American Book Award, a New England Literary Lights Award, and the Myers Outstanding Book Award. In addition, MacDonald has been a guest columnist for the *Boston Globe*'s Op-Ed page.

As an activist, he focused his efforts in the 1990s on cross-cultural coalition building to reduce violence. He founded Boston's successful gun buyback program (1992–97), which took 2,900 working firearms off the streets. He also started the South Boston Vigil Group (1996), which gave a public voice to that neighborhood's survivors of violence and the drug trade.

He has received residencies at Blue Mountain Center, the MacDowell Colony, and the Djerassi Artist Residency Program; he was granted a Bellagio Center Fellowship through the Rockefeller Foundation. He lives in Brooklyn, New York, and teaches writing at Northeastern University in Boston.

ELAINE TYLER MAY, Regents Professor of American studies and history at the University of Minnesota, received her Ph.D. in U.S. history from the University of California–Los Angeles. She is president-elect of the Organization of American Historians, and she served as president of the American Studies Association in 1995–96. She has taught at Princeton University, Harvard University, and University College, Dublin, Ireland. Her publications include *Great Expectations: Marriage and Divorce in Post-Victorian America* (1980); *Homeward Bound: American Families in the Cold War Era* (3rd ed., 2008); *Pushing the Limits: American Women, 1940–1961* (1996); and *Barren in the Promised Land: Childless Americans and the Pursuit of Happiness* (1997). She is also coauthor of a college-level textbook, *Created Equal: A History of the United States* (3rd ed., 2008). She has written for the *New York Times*, the *Los Angeles Times*, and several journals and has been featured on National Public Radio and public television and in several documentaries.

CHERI REGISTER's *Packinghouse Daughter* (2000), a memoir about growing up working class in a Minnesota meatpacking town, won a Minnesota Book Award and an American Book Award (2001) and was a BookSense 76 selection; its opening chapter was listed as a Notable Essay in *Best American Essays*. Her books on international adoption, *"Are Those Kids Yours?"* (1991) and *Beyond Good Intentions: A Mother Reflects on Raising Internationally Adopted Children* (2005), provide perspective and challenge the conventional wisdom about international adoption. She has also written *The Chronic Illness Experience: Days of Patience and Passion* (1987, reissued 1999) and many essays, articles, and book reviews. She is a teaching fellow and a master track advisor at the Loft Literary Center in Minneapolis. Her work has been supported by grants and fellowships from the Minnesota State Arts Board, the Jerome Foundation, the Dayton-Hudson Foundation, the Minnesota Historical Society, the Loft Literary Center, the American-Scandinavian Foundation, and the Swedish Council on Humanities and Literary Research.

D. J. WALDIE is the author of *Holy Land: A Suburban Memoir* (1996), *Real City: Downtown Los Angeles Inside/Out* (2001), *Where We Are Now:*

Notes from Los Angeles (2004), *Close to Home: An American Album* (2004), and *California Romantica* (2007). *Holy Land* received the California Book Award for nonfiction in 1996. Selections from *Holy Land* were included in the Library of America anthology *Writing from Los Angeles* in 2003. In 2004, *Where We Are Now* was named one of the best books of the year by the *Los Angeles Times Book Review*. Waldie also is a recipient of a Whiting Writers' Award. D. J. Waldie has been the public information officer for the city of Lakewood since 1978. He received a master's in comparative literature from the University of California–Irvine in 1974. He lives a not-quite-middle-class life in Lakewood, in the house his parents bought in 1946.

231

Tell Me True was designed by Will Powers at Minnesota Historical Society Press and set in type by Allan Johnson at Phoenix Type, Appleton, Minnesota. The typefaces are Whitman, designed by Kent Lew, and Kievit, designed by Michael Abbink. Printed by Thomson-Shore, Inc., Dexter, Michigan.